For the Life
of the World

Theology for the Life of the World

Jesus Christ is God come to dwell among humans, to be, to speak, and to act "for the life of the world" (John 6:51). Taking its mandate from the character and mission of God, Christian theology's task is to discern, articulate, and commend visions of flourishing life in light of God's self-revelation in Jesus Christ. The *Theology for the Life of the World* series features texts that do just that.

Human life is diverse and multifaceted, and so will be the books in this series. Some will focus on one specific aspect of life. Others will elaborate expansive visions of human persons, social life, or the world in relation to God. All will share the conviction that theology is vital to exploring the character of true life in diverse settings and orienting us toward it. No task is greater than for each of us and all of us together to discern and pursue the flourishing of all in God's creation. These books are meant as a contribution to that task.

For the Life of the World

Theology That Makes a Difference

Miroslav Volf and Matthew Croasmun

BrazosPress

a division of Baker Publishing Group
Grand Rapids, Michigan

© 2019 by Miroslav Volf and Matthew Croasmun

Published by Brazos Press
a division of Baker Publishing Group
PO Box 6287, Grand Rapids, MI 49516-6287
www.brazospress.com

Printed in the United States of America

ISBN: 978-1-58743-401-3
Library of Congress Cataloging in Publication Control Number: 2018020645

19 20 21 22 23 24 25   7 6 5 4 3 2 1

For our daughters,
Mira Frances and Junia Ruth

Contents

Introduction

Why Theology Matters—To Us

Though written in a style of an invitation, this book is a manifesto. Before we begin, we should to tell you, each in our own voice, why and how theology has come to matter to us, and then, together, we should sketch the main thesis of the book: academic theology ought to be, but today largely isn't, about what matters the most—the true life in the presence of God. The failure of theology to attend to its purpose is a loss for the church and for the world, for theology is uniquely qualified to explore what matters the most. And this is a loss for theology itself—for theology will either refocus itself on what matters the most or gradually cease to matter at all.

Volf: I grew up in a place and at a time when we, a small group of teenagers who knew no better, thought that no intellectual endeavor could possibly matter more than doing theology. The time was the early 1970s. The place was Tito's Yugoslavia and, for me specifically, a house in Novi Sad at the end of a dirt road—in fact, two small rooms that my father, a confectioner-turned-Pentecostal-minister, had built in its courtyard with his own hands. From its windows, through low-hanging branches of a cherry tree, I had a fine view of an electrical substation at the edge of a swamp.

A few years after I ceased to guiltily delight in the sound of the swamp's large and unsuspecting toads exploding and then going belly up when hit by the stone from my slingshot, I started spending days and nights in one of these two makeshift rooms reading the Bible, C. S. Lewis, Plato, Bertrand Russell (yes, go figure!), and, later, Karl Barth, Rudolf Bultmann, Wolfhart Pannenberg, Simone Weil, and Joseph Ratzinger—and teaching myself English and Greek in the process. I was part of a small group of young theological enthusiasts. Except for its oldest and most zealous member, who had read the entire Bible, cover to cover, thirteen times in the first year of his faith journey, all of us were, roughly, halfway through high school.

For us, theology was about the unbreakable tie between human transcendent longing and our mundane strivings, about the power of Jesus Christ, the Word of God and the Lamb of God, which stood in irreconcilable contrast to the power of soldiers, ideologues, bureaucrats, and secret service agents; it was about the right of persons—about *our* right, too, of course—to determine the shape and the direction of their individual and social lives, rather than, like some wound-up tin soldiers, to simply march in unison to the drumbeat of a failing revolution. Theology was about a new world coming from God and in God's way, a new social order whose creation and survival wouldn't demand thousands on thousands of dead as did the order in which we were born—my own father having come a hair's breadth from becoming one of them. In short, theology was about the truth and beauty of human existence in a world of justice, peace, and joy. For us, no endeavor could matter more than doing good theology—though for me personally getting hold of a pair of US-made Levi's bell-bottom jeans, Italian platform shoes, and a tight-fitting Indian gauze shirt wasn't far behind in importance.

As we spent our days and nights (yes, lots of long nights) reading and arguing about all matters theological, we had no idea that out in the wide world of Western academies, where we all wanted to study, theology was in a serious crisis.

Volf and Croasmun: Like disoriented and impoverished descendants of a monarch long deposed, some of us theologians live under a cloud of doom and futility, nostalgic for the glory and power of our ancestors but hopeless about the future. Theology had its time, but that time is no more. It would have been better, we think, had we given up long ago on the untimely endeavor and devoted our energies to more reputable academic pursuits or some more useful activity.

Others among us feel like impoverished but proud aristocrats, with fraying clothes and crumbling dwellings but a soaring sense of self-importance. We continue to do well what theologians have always done—what we *feel* theologians have always done—but we do so with a big chip on our shoulders. If only other academics or the general public would recognize our greatness and pay attention to the fruits of our wisdom, ancient wisdom, God's wisdom! If only some rich heiress would fall in love with us and return the proper luster to our clothes and dwellings!

Still other theologians, perhaps the majority of us, have acquired democratic sensibilities and settled into daily routines as "knowledge producers" employed by institutions that compete in global markets. We teach our courses and write reviews, scholarly articles, and an occasional book. We work hard to accomplish what it takes to get tenure (and nervously bite our nails through the process). We have a job, and we want to do it well: to add our own grain of intellectual sand to the vast metropolis of knowledge and to instruct students about a tradition that we aren't sure is truly alive anymore.

In one way or another, theologians seem to have lost theological *eros*, our sense of divine calling to grapple with the ultimate questions of human existence and of the world's destiny.

Volf: By now I have been a student of theology for forty-five years, thirty-five of them as a teacher. In a sense, I wrote this book to give myself a reason to keep faith with the dream of the teenager-theologian I once was. But my concern isn't primarily autobiographical integrity; after all, platform shoes or their current equivalents don't matter to me nearly as much now as they did then. My concern is the self-marginalizing and self-defeating response of theologians to the obsession with acquisition of resources and entertainment in the broader culture and especially to the dominance of the sciences in modern universities. Along with other scholars in the humanities, we theologians have sought to recast our discipline so as to acquire a legitimate home in the great edifice of science, but instead we have "dug a hole and pitched [ourselves] to its bottom."[1] The price we paid for the right to make at best marginal additions to the storehouse of knowledge was the loss of the ability to address the most profound and important questions of human existence, which the sciences, by the very nature of their methodologies, are unable even to take up, let alone to answer. I became a student of theology in search of true life in the midst of a false one; I am a theologian now for that same reason. This book explains why and invites others to join the endeavor.

Croasmun: The most theological thing I have ever done was to plant a church—a community in which Bible scholars, ethicists, philosophers, and, yes, a stray "theologian" proper, have *done* theology as we have *lived* theologically. A community in which graphic designers, poets, musicians, sociologists, and even lawyers and medical doctors have become "accidental theologians." It began almost imperceptibly and quite by accident. We should have known something theological was afoot when we found ourselves spending evenings on a back porch listening to a friend—a Christian Nietzsche scholar perched, with not a hint of ironic self-consciousness, on a stump in the backyard—call us to live lives that amounted to more than a never-ending quest for ever-greater degrees of comfort. I remember waking up at 3:30 a.m. to walk with that friend three miles across town to the train station—simply because walking was more life-giving than driving and the conversation along the way was worth the effort. Summer evenings were spent poring over Karl Barth, Søren Kierkegaard, C. S. Lewis, Kwame Bediako, Marilynne Robinson, and, yes, Nietzsche, with

---

1. Anthony Kronman, *Education's End: Why Our Colleges and Universities Have Given Up on the Meaning of Life* (New Haven: Yale University Press, 2007), 139.

the visceral sense that our lives depended on the words on the pages.

The questions of life were theological because theology was the question of life. Where to live—and with whom—was a theological question. We bought houses together; we shared cars. How and whether to own at all was a theological question. Rhythms of work and rest were a matter of deep theological reflection. Art and beauty were perhaps among the most theological questions of all. Theology was a question about the nature of the life we were living *together*. We read 1 Corinthians as if it were addressed to us as we wondered how to be a community that functioned collectively to discern the voice of God. The transgressive nature of the kingdom in the life and teaching of Jesus led our small, evangelical church to cross religious boundaries and discern God's voice speaking to us—*teaching* us—through our Muslim and secular humanist neighbors. Galatians became a field manual for navigating questions of difference as we struggled with what it meant to become in actuality the multiethnic community we had always wanted to be. When the white leaders of our church handed over senior leadership to a black man, whom God clearly called to be our pastor, Jonathan's words in 1 Samuel explained what our white leaders experienced: "I will be second," said Jonathan (1 Sam. 23:17)—and we have been blessed to be so. Theology mattered.

Whether the *scholarship* we did every day mattered the same way was less clear. Those of us who were doctoral students at the time were being trained to become knowledge-workers rather than wisdom-seekers. Theology that gave life could only be whispered in the margins. True life in academia seemed to require, if not misdirection, at least *indirection*—and the fact that most of us were aiming at theology only indirectly (through biblical studies or history or philosophy) suggests we had already learned our lessons well. These other fields promised the chance to generate real knowledge, which was certainly more reliable professional capital than true life. Respectable theology was something quite separate from true life—in fact, it might make true life impossible. Early on in my program I was told what to expect during my studies:

after two years of coursework, amid taking exams, teaching, and writing the dissertation prospectus, usually, if one was married, there then followed *divorce*. Gallows humor, no doubt, but even clever gallows kill.

This book is a chance, early in my professional life, to make a case for the guild I'm joining to set its eyes on theology that yields beautiful, abundant, transgressive, and reconciling *life*. Not that guild theology should naively become church theology. But perhaps guild theology would benefit from being tugged toward church theology's *telos*. And, even more, given the love that my "respectable theology" (biblical studies) has given me for the humanities of the modern pluralistic university, my hope between the lines in this book is that guild theology might call the university to become a place where we learn to discern the good life together across important and enduring lines of difference.

Volf and Croasmun: As an intellectual endeavor, theology matters because it is about what matters the most for human life. Theology worth its name is about what we ought to desire above all things for ourselves and for the world, about what we should desire in all the things that we desire (whether our desire is effective economic systems and just political orders, livable cities and deep friendships, possessions or lack thereof, healthy bodies and joyous progeny, or even those bell-bottom jeans and Indian gauze shirts). Theology matters because it is about the true life of the world.

The first two books of the Hebrew Bible draw an arc from the creation of the world, over the abyss of the world's self-destructive sin and Israel's forced labor in Egypt, to the establishment of God's covenant and of God's dwelling place among the people called to be a "royal priesthood." The New Testament, from its first book to its last, redraws that arc to include at its endpoint humanity and the world in their entirety: with the birth of Jesus Christ, a descendant of David and the seed of Abraham, God has come to dwell among humans so as to make "all things new" and turn the entire world into God's home and our home in one (Rev. 21:3, 5). This book is a call to those of us who see ourselves as theologians—academic theologians, church theologians, lay theologians, accidental theologians, any kind of theologian—to dare to believe that "God's home" is the ultimate goal of human striving and the ultimate object of human rejoicing and therefore to make God's home and the world's journey to it the main focus of our most rigorous thinking and honest truth-seeking.

Humanity today faces many challenges: the risks of an unprecedented pace of technological development; seemingly irreversible ecological degradation; immense discrepancies in wealth, knowledge, and power among individuals and the peoples of the world; an inability to live in peace given our manifold differences; and more. As we write this, the symbolic Doomsday Clock of the *Bulletin of the Atomic Scientists* is set on two minutes before midnight. But the first step toward ecological, economic, and political health is conversion—reaffirmation or rediscovery of our human purpose and setting ourselves on a journey toward it. Even if it were true, as dystopian literature and some scientific predictions suggest, that humanity is entering a valley of dry bones of our own making—desolate landscapes, cities in ruin, people at war over basic resources—we will be able to live with dignity in that valley, too, only if we know who we are and what our purpose is. And we'll need that same knowledge inscribed into the very character of our souls in order to get out of that valley.

———

We have nothing against writing treatises—even long ones, in multiple tomes—but this book is not a treatise. It is a manifesto. In writing it, we implicitly request not simply that you "take and read." Instead, we ask you to "do something": change the way you do theology and help change the way others do it as well. Of course, we want you to read the book and read it carefully; we want you to debate its contents and debate them vigorously. But as you do, keep in mind that it is a manifesto, written in a style that proceeds in large steps over vast intellectual spaces. Every sentence, even every clause, could have been a page, with equally long footnotes. Whether you find yourself agreeing, disagreeing, qualifying, or doing a bit of all three, keep moving along. By the time you have reached the end, we'd like to see you committed to doing theology for the life of the world. Theology practiced as a specialized vocation is a means—an important, even an indispensable means, but a means nonetheless. We will have reached our goal in writing the book if it generates serious discussion about how doing theology fits into the grand goal of God: fashioning each human and the entire world into God's home and our true home as well.

The structure of the book speaks for itself. We start by arguing that the true, good, or flourishing life is the fundamental human question, neglected today but more urgent than ever (chap. 1). We then propose that the current crisis of theology—a discipline that over the centuries placed the question of the flourishing life at the center of its concern—stems largely from its failure, especially in recent decades, to wrestle confidently with this question (chap. 2). In chapter 3, the center of the book, we call theologians to make this the main purpose of theology: discerning, articulating, and commending accounts of the true life, summed up for us in the image of "God's home among humans." In chapter 4 we show how a theology of flourishing life that claims to be true for all human beings should neither exacerbate social conflict in pluralistic societies nor suppress the particularities of individual persons. To do such theology well, we argue in chapter 5, theologians need to align their lives with the basic vision of life whose shape they are discerning, articulating, and commending. The book ends with a sketch of an account of flourishing that draws on the writings of the first Christian theologian, the apostle Paul (chap. 6).

The kind of theology we are proposing requires a corresponding pedagogy. To give an account of Christian pedagogy would require another book; this one paves the way for it by sketching a vison of the goal of such a pedagogy. Theological education comes in many forms—from elementary Sunday school and confirmation classes to courses offered in Christian secondary schools and colleges to seminary training in all its varieties to the doctoral and postdoctoral educations of academic theologians. As we see it, a common aim unites these forms of theological education. Theological education is a dimension of Christian education, and it therefore shares in its goal: forming human beings according the pattern of Christ, such that each person and community is able to improvise the way of Christ in the flow of time in anticipation of becoming, along with the entire creation, the home of God.

1

The Human Quest

Christian theology has lost its way because it has neglected its purpose. We believe the purpose of theology is to discern, articulate, and commend visions of flourishing life in light of God's self-revelation in Jesus Christ. The flourishing of human beings and all God's creatures in the presence of God is God's foremost concern for creation and should therefore be the central purpose of theology. With this manifesto we aim to return theology to itself so it can better serve communities of Christian conviction and participate in truth-seeking cultural conversation about flourishing life for all.

The theology that has lost its way is above all professional, academic theology, which is only a subset of Christian theology as a whole. In an important sense, all Christians are theologians. As Christians, we seek to think and speak plausibly about our journeys with Christ into our own and the world's fullness, to make the practice of faith coherent.[1] Call this "everyday theology."[2] From

1. See Rowan Williams, *On Christian Theology* (Oxford: Blackwell, 2000), xii.
2. To claim that Christian theology is integrally related to the practice of the faith is not to discount the contributions non-Christians make to Christian

the beginning, in the very earliest Christian communities, however, doing theology was not only a general practice but also a special calling. The apostles and teachers were the first theologians. Call this "church theology." In the course of the history of Christianity, theologians were gradually distinguished from teachers, and, in more recent centuries, theology became an academic discipline, even a disciplinary specialization (as when "theologians" are distinguished from biblical scholars, church historians, or ethicists). People who engage in such specialized activity are "professional" or more narrowly "academic" theologians. It is about them and their activity—it is about us and our activity, as both writers are theologians in this sense—that we are primarily concerned in this book. We use "theology" primarily to designate this special calling to understand the practice of faith.[3]

In the second chapter, we describe the contemporary crisis of theology. Starting with the third chapter, we offer a proposal for its renewal, arguing for the version of theology whose purpose is to discern, articulate, and commend visions of flourishing life. In

theology—scholars working in religious studies, philosophy, history, anthropology, and the like, and sometimes on the faculties of Christian theological schools themselves. Their work is crucial to understanding Christianity and the world more broadly, and, like any good interlocutor, serves to inform the descriptive and normative claims that Christian theologians make. We live in a pluralistic world, and Christian theology is, as we argue, one among many contending sets of voices that articulate and commend a vision of flourishing life. Those who advocate alternative visions and offer critiques of, or friendly amendments to, Christian visions play fruitful roles in this contestation about the nature of the *true life*.

3. Those called to be theologians—church theologians and academic theologians—should pay special attention to theological work going on among Christian intellectuals who would not ordinarily call themselves theologians. Some Christians are extraordinary thinkers—philosophers, historians, writers, transdisciplinary intellectuals, scientists, and more—and they often bring their thinking to bear on the Christian way of life. Leaning on the work of Elizabeth Dreyer (*Accidental Theologians: Four Women Who Shaped Christianity* [Cincinnati: Franciscan Media, 2014]), Christian Wiman calls these Christians "accidental theologians" and includes among them figures such as Fyodor Dostoevsky, Simone Weil, and Vincent van Gogh; Wiman himself is an exceptionally good accidental theologian! See above all *My Bright Abyss: Meditation of a Modern Believer* (New York: Farrar, Straus and Giroux, 2013).

this chapter, we explain in broad and formal terms what we mean by "flourishing life" and why and how the question of flourishing life matters today. This is a book about the future of Christian theology, but Christian theology is about an issue that concerns all human beings in a fundamental way.

Why "Flourishing Life"?

By "flourishing life" we mean the good toward which humans are meant to strive. It names not so much any number of things we desire, but the ultimate goal of our striving along with the values that determine what is truly worth desiring. We use the term more or less interchangeably with "true life," "good life," "life worth living," "human fullness," "life that truly is life," and more. Though "the good life" is a technical term in classical philosophy and in the Christian theology that developed in conversation with it, we prefer "flourishing life" because it is universal in scope, tying the good life of humans to the good life of all God's creatures, and because it avoids the popular connotations of "good life" that evoke images of extravagant consumption.[4] Granted, "flourishing" can conjure visions of life aloof from hardship and oppression, so we will sometimes use "true life" to make space for the arduous forms that the best of human lives will often have to take on this side of the full realization of God's new creation and under the conditions of sin. Each of these terms has its own intellectual

4. As far as we can tell, the term "human flourishing" was coined by Elizabeth Anscombe in something akin to the sense we use here in her landmark essay "Modern Moral Philosophy," *Philosophy* 33, no. 124 (January 1958): 1–19. Forty years later, Mary Grey proposed "a theology of flourishing for the next millennium" in "Survive or Thrive? A Theology of Flourishing for the Next Millennium," *Studies: An Irish Quarterly Review* 88, no. 352 (Winter 1999): 396–407, writing in an ecofeminist tradition that included the philosophical work of Chris J. Cuomo, *Feminism and Ecological Communities: An Ethic of Flourishing* (New York: Routledge, 1998), and the theological work of Grace M. Jantzen, "Feminism and Flourishing: Gender and Metaphor in Feminist Theology," *Feminist Theology* 4, no. 10 (September 1, 1995): 81–101.

pedigree in the broad tradition of reflection on human nature, destiny, and place in the world. For us, the Christian faith and not the intellectual pedigree of the term decisively shapes the character of flourishing life.

Sometimes visions of flourishing are like vivid images we are able to see and describe, but more often they are like a lens through which we see everything—the tacit "background" against which we live our lives, as Charles Taylor puts it.[5] If they are only implicit, we need to tease them out, make them explicit. In either case, it is our human responsibility to reflect on their function, origin, content, and existential or intellectual adequacy because they define our world and our very selves. We can switch from one vision to another, but if we do so in reality and not just in imagination, we become a "new person": we come to experience ourselves and our world in a different way, and our lives take a new turn.

A Centuries-Long Concern

For much of humanity's early history, human beings saw their ultimate good in natural forms of well-being: health, wealth, fertility, and longevity. During what some philosophers and sociologists have described as "axial transformations," a sense of the inadequacy of such natural accounts of human flourishing crystallized.[6] Today's world religions emerged out of these transformations. Each stands for an alternative to the idea that the ultimate good consists

5. Charles Taylor takes up the language of Wittgenstein, Heidegger, and Polanyi. Charles Taylor, *A Secular Age* (Cambridge, MA: Belknap, 2007), 13–14.

6. Karl Jaspers, in *Vom Ursprung und Ziel der Geschichte* (Zürich: Artemis, 1949), introduced the idea of axiality—he used the term "axial age"—to public discussion after World War II. We prefer the language of "axial transformations" (so also many authors in the collection of essays *The Axial Age and Its Consequences*, ed. Robert N. Bellah and Hans Joas [Cambridge, MA: Harvard University Press, 2012]) to indicate that we are after a heuristic distinction between preaxial and postaxial societies, without implying some of Jaspers's historical claims about an axial age. Our invocation of this language is close to Charles Taylor's (*Secular Age*, 792n9). For an English translation of Jaspers's work, see Karl Jaspers, *The Origin and Goal of History*, trans. Michael Bullock (New Haven: Yale University Press, 1953).

in forms of natural well-being. Each in its own way distinguishes between mundane and transcendent realms, and each in its own way claims that the ultimate human good consists in alignment of self (and, for some traditions, the world) with the transcendent order. At the heart of the great world religions lies an answer to the question of the true life, the good life, the genuinely flourishing life.

World religions provide the most enduring, most widespread, and, arguably, still most potent visions of human flourishing. But religions are not the only source of such visions. For many great philosophers, an articulation of the good life is a central concern,[7] either the pivot around which their philosophies turn or an indispensable theme of their philosophies. This is true, for instance, of Socrates, Plato, Aristotle, Spinoza, Hume, Kant, Hegel, Kierkegaard, Marx, Mill, Nietzsche, Murdoch, and Weil. In recent centuries, some philosophers have come to advocate modern and secular versions of the preaxial account of the human good centered on health, wealth, fertility, and longevity.[8] Nietzsche might be the most radical among them, as he contests all forms of the distinction between mundane and transcendent realms,[9] whether the distinction is drawn between sensible and supersensible worlds (as in Plato and monotheistic religions, for instance) or within the sensible world (as in Karl Marx and some forms of secular

7. In their own way, many great writers have pursued the same project. Referring to Dostoevsky, and indirectly to himself, David Foster Wallace wrote, "His concern was always what it means to be a human being." David Foster Wallace, "Joseph Frank's Dostoevsky," in *Consider the Lobster, and Other Essays* (New York: Little, Brown, 2006), 255–74, here 265. On Wallace and the question of the good life, see Nathan Ballantyne and Justin Tosi, "David Foster Wallace on the Good Life," in *Freedom and the Self: Essays on the Philosophy of David Foster Wallace*, ed. Steven M. Cahn and Maureen Eckert (New York: Columbia University Press, 2015), 133–64.

8. For a recent example of taking up the question of meaningful life that finds inspiration in preaxial forms of thought, see Hubert Dreyfus and Sean Dorrance Kelly, *All Things Shining: Reading the Western Classics to Find Meaning in a Secular Age* (New York: Free Press, 2011), 58–87, 190–223.

9. On Nietzsche's rejection of "two worlds," see Friedrich Nietzsche, *The Will to Power*, trans. Walter Kaufmann and R. J. Hollingdale (New York: Random House, 1968), 507.

humanism, for instance). Still, he too had a vision of the kinds of human beings he wanted to see "bred."[10]

Though the world's religions and philosophers offer diverse visions of the flourishing life, these visions, we propose, share three formal features—that is, flourishing life has a tripartite structure.[11] Each world religion or philosophy gives an account of life going well, life led well, and life feeling as it should. Life going well refers to the "circumstantial" dimension of the flourishing life, to the desirable circumstances of life—be they natural (like fertile, uncontaminated land), social (like a just political order or a good reputation), or personal (like health and longevity). Life led well refers to the "agential" dimension of the flourishing life, to the good conduct of life—from right thoughts of the heart and right acts to right habits and virtues. Life feeling as it should is about the "affective" dimension of the flourishing life, about states of "happiness" (contentment, joy) and empathy. Each of the three features has its own integrity, but each is not like a leg of some "good-life stool" bearing separately the weight. Instead, each is also tied to the others, both influencing them and being influenced by them.

This, then, is what we mean by a vision of flourishing life: a set of explicit or implicit convictions about what it means for us to lead life well, for our life to go well, and for it to feel right, convictions that guide—or should guide—all our desires and efforts. The Christian faith, centered as it is on the divine Word become flesh in Jesus Christ as the true life and light of the world, is such a vision. Or, rather, it is a large and often quarrelsome family of such visions. Christian theology ought to be, above all, about critically discerning, articulating, and commending this vision. With this goal, theologians ought to enter the centuries-long and global conversation in which religious and nonreligious thinkers

10. Friedrich Nietzsche, *The Anti-Christ*, in *"The Anti-Christ," "Ecce Homo," "Twilight of the Idols," and Other Writings*, ed. Aaron Ridley and Judith Norman, trans. Judith Norman (Cambridge: Cambridge University Press, 2005), §3, p. 4.

11. For one Christian account of the tripartite structure of the flourishing life—that of the apostle Paul—see chap. 6.

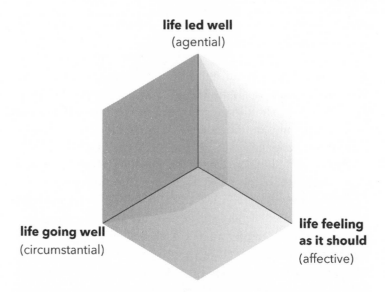

life led well
(agential)

life going well
(circumstantial)

**life feeling
as it should**
(affective)

Figure 1.1 The tripartite formal structure of flourishing life.

wrestle with the most important human question: What is the true, flourishing life, and how can we live it?

But why? Aren't there other issues we ought to attend to, both more pressing and perhaps more manageable than this biggest of all big questions, like various forms of exclusion or exploitation? Or can't we just assume a Christian vision of flourishing as given and go on with the endeavor of living it?

A Pearl of Great Price

Some dismiss exploration of the good life as a luxury, a matter of "extra credit" we can take up if so inclined after the necessities of life—food, shelter, and safety—have been secured, and secured for all. It is a mistake, however, to suppose that the satisfaction of basic needs can be separated from the meaning and goodness of life. Basic needs are famously difficult to pin down. Beyond the resources human beings require as biological organisms, the very determination of what constitutes a basic human need depends not just on the social standing of a person but decisively also on the kind of life we find worth desiring.[12] Moreover, cultural, economic, and political struggle against deprivation and oppression will fail if a positive vision of flourishing life doesn't guide it. That's why, according to the Gospels, Jesus didn't just feed the poor and heal the sick, although he did that and stated explicitly that he came to do that; more importantly, he called them to reorient their entire lives around seeking God and God's righteousness.[13]

We insult the humanity of the languishing when we suggest that concern with the basic character and direction of their lives is somehow beyond their reach, that they have to progress on the hierarchy of needs—from food, shelter, and safety to community to self-esteem—until they are finally capable of reflecting on the meaning and puzzling out the shape of true life. An eight-year-old girl getting up before dawn to take the one family cow to pasture before going to school (like Miroslav's mother did as a child) can ask it no less than can a respected scientist working in an industry

---

12. On "necessities" as a social category, Adam Smith says the following:
By necessaries I understand not only the commodities which are indispensably necessary for the support of life, but whatever the custom of the country renders it indecent for creditable people, even of the lowest order, to be without. A linen shirt, for example, is, strictly speaking, not a necessary of life. The Greeks and Romans lived, I suppose, very comfortably though they had no linen. But in the present times, through the greater part of Europe, a creditable day-labourer would be ashamed to appear in public without a linen shirt, the want of which would be supposed to denote that disgraceful degree of poverty which, it is presumed, nobody can well fall into without extreme bad luck. (Adam Smith, *An Inquiry into the Nature and Causes of the Wealth of Nations* 5.2.2.4, ed. Edwin Cannan [New York: Random House, 1994], 938–39)
For a contemporary approach, see Martha C. Nussbaum, *Creating Capabilities: The Human Development Approach* (Cambridge, MA: Harvard University Press, 2011).

13. Cf. Matt. 6:33. Working within Marxist tradition, many years ago Paulo Freire made a compelling argument that a positive vision of human fullness is indispensable for liberation. Without grabbing hold of a vision of a "new man" or a "fuller humanity," the liberated oppressed are likely to become "sub-oppressors": "Their ideal is to be men; but for them, to be men is to be oppressors. This is their model of humanity." Paulo Freire, *Pedagogy of the Oppressed* (London: Bloomsbury, 2014), 45–47.

(like Matt's father did). Those wracked by pain because of illness, suffering under the yoke of oppression, or worrying about their next meal need—and often *feel* the need for—visions of human fullness at least as much as and sometimes more than those who are healthy, unconstrained, and well fed.[14] Many originators of great, ancient visions of human flourishing as well as the majority of those who embraced them through the centuries lived in circumstances most people in economically developed nations today would describe as dire. Suffering of one kind or another and the indignities that accompany it have been historically and continue to be presently the main motor for both the search for a vision of life that is truly worthy of human beings and for the struggle, personal and social, to turn that vision into reality.

A compelling vision of flourishing life is not a luxury, a cozy reading room for a middle-class home that already has a kitchen, bathroom, living space, and bedrooms. It is a basic need for a being who does not and cannot live by bread alone. All human beings in all cultures, each in their own way, aspire to genuine flourishing, their own and that of those they care for. First, we are inescapably oriented toward some good—toward things, states of affairs, practices, and emotions we perceive as good. Second, we are reflective and moral beings. We want to know that the good we strive toward is in fact desirable. Finally, aware as we are of living in time, we gather our past in memory and our future in anticipation, and we want to be assured of the goodness or rightness of our whole life. Unless the speed and noise of life are unrelenting and entertainment beguilingly captivating, we will occasionally survey our life—past, present, and future—and ask what it would mean for the entirety to be "good."

Truly flourishing life is the most important concern of our lives, the pearl for which it's worth selling everything else we might have—wealth, power, fame, or pleasure (Matt. 13:45–46). With that pearl, we receive back improved many of the goods we've sold to acquire it; without that pearl, we ourselves are diminished

14. See Grey, "Survive or Thrive?," 402–3.

and lost, and none of the goods we refused to sell in order to acquire it can make up for the damage. But like the swine of Jesus's Sermon on the Mount (Matt. 7:6), many of us, ordinary people and intellectuals alike, and especially those in the affluent West, trample that pearl under our feet, seeing in it nothing fit to satisfy our wayward hunger.

Choosing a Vision for Life

Today, more than at any previous time in history, the character of flourishing life is a pressing concern, especially, perhaps, when we fail to experience it as such. Though the issue is ancient and basic, as we have seen, we now ask it and have to answer it in a new way. In ages past as in some traditional cultures today, a vision of the good life was largely inscribed into the objective conditions of lived lives—in the perceived givenness of the cosmic and social orders, in accepted religious rituals and traditions, in how communities engaged in the cultural, economic, and political reproduction of life. Even individuals' vocations were mostly passed from mother to daughter and from father to son. Though they often sensed the need to discern the specific shape of their particular life, most people believed that the ultimate direction of life and the "tables of values" (to borrow a phrase from Friedrich Nietzsche) from which their lives gained shape and significance were pregiven, perhaps even "natural." For a large and increasing portion of the world's population, this is no longer the case.

Free to Choose, Forced to Choose

In cultures shaped by modernity, we have come to live "disembedded" lives.[15] No longer experiencing ourselves as constituents of a meaningful cosmos and members of a social body, we modern

15. Taylor, *Secular Age*, 146–58. Taylor describes *both* disembedding that has happened as part of axial transformations *and* modern disembedding that is

human beings imagine ourselves and act first and foremost as individuals, ideally sovereign owners of ourselves and our actions. We can no longer "read off" meaning from our social and cosmic locations. Nothing has claim to our allegiance until we first choose to give it our allegiance. We live under what many years ago Peter Berger described as a "heretical imperative": we are not just free to choose but are forced to do so.[16] As a consequence, what counts as flourishing life and what it means specifically for each person to flourish require from us intentional deliberation.[17]

As we will see shortly, we tend not to spend much time on the matter but either float along in a Lazy River or paddle madly in the boulder-riddled rapids to beat others to the finish line.[18] Still, we float and paddle in a cultural river with many currents and crosscurrents. When we become reflective about our lives, we must contend with those diverse currents, and we are forced to choose or reconfirm the choices we have made. Even a birth into a rich tradition that initially defines the flourishing life for us doesn't relieve us from choice. Instead of simply taking on and living out a preset vision of flourishing—perhaps struggling but failing to live it or chafing against it—we are pushed to always engage afresh the question of *which* life is, in fact, good.

Let's remind ourselves of the nature of the choice we are talking about. To choose here is not so much to pick one among many of more or less desirable things. It is to opt for the direction of our entire life, either to confirm the course we are on—which we enact

---

in some sense an extension of the axial of disembedding, especially its Christian form.

16. Peter Berger, *The Heretical Imperative: Contemporary Possibilities of Religious Affirmation* (Garden City, NY: Anchor, 1979). See also Charles Taylor, *Secular Age*; Charles Taylor, *Varieties of Religion Today: William James Revisited* (Cambridge, MA: Harvard University Press, 2002).

17. For the importance of "meaning," "an essentially modern predicament," see Charles Taylor, *Sources of the Self: The Making of the Modern Identity* (Cambridge, MA: Harvard University Press, 1989), 10, 16–19.

18. We take the metaphor of the Lazy River from Zadie Smith, "The Lazy River," *New Yorker*, December 18 and 25, 2017, 94–97, https://www.newyorker.com/magazine/2017/12/18/the-lazy-river.

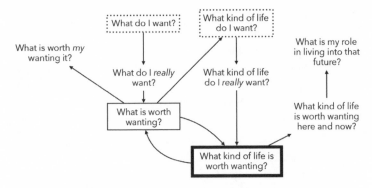

Figure 1.2 Our presenting questions about particular desires ("What do I want?") and our desires for the shape of our life as a whole ("What kind of life do I want?") ultimately lead us to the fundamental question of the good life ("What kind of life is worth wanting?") and return to us more refined versions of our presenting questions.

without much thought in the myriad daily choices we make—or to change the course of our lives. Put more abstractly, we are deciding among candidates for the character and purpose of our lives and for the tables of values or "reflexive standards" by which we evaluate our ordinary choices.[19] We are deciding what kind of human being it is worth being and what kind of world it is worth inhabiting.

For a century and a half or so, many in the West were convinced that, when it comes to a vision of flourishing life, the main choice in the West, and increasingly around the globe, was between some form of religious faith and secularism. Secularism seemed to be winning, in fact. But the situation has proven more complicated. Globally, religions, particularly Buddhism, Christianity, and Islam, continue to grow in absolute and relative terms, shape the private and public lives of billions, and spread throughout the world.[20] For most people today, the choice is not between religious faith and lack of it; it is among many forms of religious faith and

19. Hans Joas, *Do We Need Religion? On the Experience of Self-Transcendence*, trans. Alex Skinner (Boulder, CO: Paradigm, 2008), 29.

20. See Miroslav Volf, *Flourishing: Why We Need Religion in a Globalized World* (New Haven: Yale University Press, 2015), 61–62.

nonreligious philosophies of life. Multiple visions of flourishing life—mutually contending though rarely completely incompatible and each explicitly or implicitly claiming to stand for the true life—vie for the allegiance of all. We are choosing in a postsecular and pluralistic world.

Free to choose and at the same time saddled with the necessity of doing so, we are also faced with the choice between a meaningful life and life bereft of meaning. Many who see themselves as living in the shadow of what Nietzsche called "the death of God"[21] embrace the idea, with either resignation or courage, that they can give no better reasons for their basic choices than their preference itself.[22] But to choose something just because we want to is to empty our choice of significance. Any meaning that we give we can take away as well; and any choice we make then seems as good as any other.[23] In some versions of the world in which preferences are kings and queens, irreligious choices become as good as religious ones, and life cannot be rescued from the threat of arbitrariness.[24] The possibility of meaninglessness, too, and not just multiple offers of visions of true and meaningful life, keeps us searching and choosing.

21. Friedrich Nietzsche, *The Gay Science: With a Prelude in Rhymes and an Appendix of Songs*, trans. Walter Kaufmann (New York: Random House, 1974), §§108, 125, 343, pp. 167, 181, 279. See also Friedrich Nietzsche, *Thus Spoke Zarathustra: A Book for All and None*, trans. Walter Kaufmann (New York: Viking, 1966), 200–201.

22. Most atheists don't think that without God we are doomed to the emptiness of a meaningless existence. In *Religion without God*, for instance, Ronald Dworkin develops a "religious" form of atheism, marked by the gratitude for the gift of being, the sacredness of human life, and the objective beauty and goodness of nature. Ronald Dworkin, *Religion without God* (Cambridge, MA: Harvard University Press, 2013).

23. For a recent version of such a reading of our predicament and a secular suggestion about how to overcome it, see Dreyfus and Kelly, *All Things Shining*.

24. This arbitrariness is Charles Taylor's concern in rebutting the views of naive "boosters" of the authenticity ethic. Without some horizon of significance, "choice" (the lone hyper-good on this facile account of authenticity) is evacuated of all meaning and thereby fails to function as a hyper-good. Charles Taylor, *The Ethics of Authenticity* (Cambridge, MA: Harvard University Press, 1991), 31–42.

Follow Your Dream!

With multiple competing accounts of flourishing life vying for our allegiance while each tries to ward off nihilism, the question of the flourishing life is now more open—and more pressing—than ever. Yet just at this moment, serious engagement with this question is ebbing.

For one, our lives seem too crowded—too busy, we might say, were it not that after long hours of work we let entertainment and various addictions gobble up a good portion of the remaining time—to allow us to give sustained attention to the challenge of discerning the life truly worth living. David Foster Wallace describes well the predicament of people living in modern, fast-paced, and entertainment-saturated societies. It's not just that we don't know how to live meaningful lives, he says. "We don't even seem to be able to focus for very long on the question."[25]

On the rare occasions when we do focus, we are confronted with our lack of knowledge and skill to articulate for ourselves a vision of the good life. In the Life Worth Living course we teach at Yale College, a student, exasperated with the predicament in which he found himself, remarked, "The world's greatest traditions have been trying to answer this question for 3,000+ years. And now I'm supposed to work out my own answer—in my spare time?!" With neither skills nor tools to tackle the question, we resort to the habits we have learned in making consumer choices: we consult our gut feelings and some "life projects" equivalent of consumer reports, and we decide—provisionally, for the most part, always keeping our options open. Too often our hearts, which simply want what they want and are persuaded that they would wrong themselves if they didn't get it, make the decision for us. Our only master seems to be our taste, supposedly authentically ours and yet consistently mirroring what is around us.[26]

---

25. Dreyfus and Kelly, *All Things Shining*, 30, citing a Charlie Rose interview of David Foster Wallace (available at https://www.youtube.com/watch?v=hm9 4gUBCih8).

26. On taste, see Tom Vanderbilt, *You May Also Like: Taste in an Age of Endless Choice* (New York: Knopf, 2016).

But it isn't just that we are too busy and inept to take on the responsibility for the direction of our lives. In the course of modernity, the notion of the good life has been privatized. "If a kid asks what to do with his or her life," writes Hartmut Rosa, "teachers, friends, and family will be sure to offer their advice, but they will almost inevitably rush to add: 'Just find out for yourself, listen to your heart, come to know your talents and your yearnings.' Thus, the good life has become the most intimately private matter."[27] The gist of the advice is simple: "Follow your dream!" We believe that we ought to decide for ourselves how to live. More, we are convinced that the vision of life that is good for us is encoded in our particular character as individuals; an inviolable criterion of the good life is that it is authentically ours. Our choice about the matter is worthy of respect just because it is ours and resonates with who we perceive ourselves to be.

Not so long ago, we considered the founders of religions and great philosophers who thought deeply about the question of life worth living as medical doctors and nutritionists of our humanity: we expected them to tell us what human wholeness is and what's good for achieving it and why, and if we disagreed, we argued back, telling them where and why they were wrong. Now we relate to them as we do to waiters in a restaurant, whom we count on to describe each dish but not to tell us what would be good for us to order, let alone what true health is and how the meal we are about to order relates to it; in fact, we half expect them to praise any choice we make, for every choice is by definition good—as long as we like the dish! No religious figure, no philosopher, no scientist can know what kind of life is good— certainly not good for us. We alone are the true experts of how our talents and yearnings conjoin to give birth to our dreams, which legitimize our striving.

27. Hartmut Rosa, "Two Versions of the Good Life and Two Forms of Fear: Dynamic Stabilization and Resonance Conception of the Good Life," paper presented at the Yale Center for Faith and Culture conference on Joy, Security, and Fear, New Haven, CT, November 8–9, 2017, 6.

The Resources for Living Your Dream

Though silent about the nature of the good life, modern cultures are very clear, even strident, about the preconditions for the life each of us considers to be good: "Secure the resources you might need for living your dream (whatever that might be)!" Hartmut Rosa calls this the "overruling rational imperative of modernity."[28] Whatever you end up choosing as your good in the course of life, you will be better off if you accumulate economic, social, cultural, symbolic, and bodily capital—in other words, if you are rich, emotionally intelligent, educated, well connected, and good looking.[29] We invest most of our time and energy securing these resources; they make it possible for us to pursue our dreams, not just today but also tomorrow, when we, our world, and our dreams might be very different from today. Rosa offers an image of our situation: "In a way, we moderns resemble a painter who is forever concerned about improving his materials—the colors and brushes, the air condition and lighting, the canvas and easel, etc.—but never really starts to paint."[30] The means have become ends.

Perhaps another image is apt as well: when the means for life have become the ends of life, the dog has started chasing its tail.[31] To chase one's tail is bad enough; to have to chase it faster than anyone else verges on madness, yet this seems to be our situation. The resources we think we need to live the good life are competi-

28. Rosa, "Two Versions," 7.

29. See Pierre Bourdieu, *Distinction: A Social Critique of the Judgement of Taste*, trans. Richard Nice (London: Routledge, 1984).

30. Rosa, "Two Versions," 7.

31. On the phenomenon of means becoming ends, see John Stuart Mill, "Utilitarianism," in *On Liberty, and Other Essays*, ed. John Gray (Oxford: Oxford University Press, 1998), 170–71. On money as means-become-ends see Karl Marx, "Economic and Philosophical Manuscripts," in *Karl Marx: Selected Writings*, ed. David McLellan, 2nd ed. (New York: Oxford University Press, 2000), 109–11; Karl Marx, "The General Formula for Money," in *Das Kapital: A Critique of Political Economy*, vol. 1, trans. Ben Fowkes (New York: Penguin, 1990), 247–57. See also Thomas Aquinas, *Summa Theologiae* I-II.2.1: "For wealth . . . is sought for the sake of something else. . . . Consequently it cannot be man's last end."

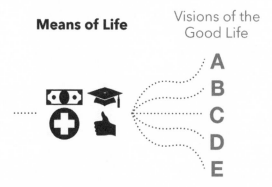

Figure 1.3 We tend to let the means of life, required to realize any vision of the flourishing life, become the purpose of our lives.

tive goods. It is not just that it is better to have more of them than to have less; we need to have more of them than our competitors do: more wealth, better education, more fame, better looks, more . . . We are like a painter obsessed with having better tools for her trade than any of her colleagues because she, madly, believes that superior tools themselves make her a greater painter.

In the course of modernity, we have made it our chief goal (and the main purpose of our major institutions—the state, the market, science and technology, education, and even religion) to secure the resources we think we need to live the life we want. The task of securing resources keeps us busy; we work more today than we ever have before.[32] Work is not all we do, of course. We enjoy the pleasures of life as well. For many, these pleasures are the purpose of work and of life itself. But when pleasure becomes our goal, we are in danger of becoming Nietzsche's "last men," beings "weary of all great striving and obsessed with comfort and safety, dreaming petty dreams and enjoying unsubtle pleasures, entertaining ourselves to idiocy while imagining ourselves as the

32. On the increase of weekly hours devoted to work notwithstanding all the work-saving technological advances, see Benjamin M. Friedman, "Work and Consumption in an Era of Unbalanced Technological Advance," *Journal of Evolutionary Economics* 27, no. 2 (April 2017): 221–37.

measure of humanity."[33] If we are more into competition than comfort, then we treat enjoyments as a resource; we compete in the sophistication and expense of pleasures, and if we do better than most in our comparison group, then we increase our reputational capital. Yet in work with all its achievements and in leisure with all its pleasures, we languish. That busy languishing closes our ears to the cries of the oppressed and our eyes to destruction of earth's ecological systems—and reinforces our disdain for the pearl of great price.

Private and Public Costs

With taste in charge of the direction of our lives and reason employed mainly for creation of resources for life, we are left vulnerable to a sneaking suspicion of the arbitrariness of our lives. When during a lull in activities or in a moment of crisis the little demon appears on our shoulders whispering into our ears that our work and our pleasures don't matter at all, we don't know how to get rid of it. It's not necessarily that we are committed to convictions that entail the meaninglessness of life. Worse yet, we are unaware of compelling options and have neither the wherewithal to explore them nor the intellectual and moral tools to adjudicate among them. The way we have been habituated to make choices

33. This quotation is from Volf, *Flourishing*, 199. It functions there as a summary of Nietzsche's famous text about the "last men" from *Thus Spoke Zarathustra*, the type of human beings he feared would be the end result of the development of Western civilization:

> The earth has become small, and on it hops the last man, who makes everything small. . . . "We have invented happiness," say the last men, and they blink. . . . A little poison now and then: that makes for pleasant dreams. And much poison at the end for a pleasant death. One still works, for work is a form of entertainment. But one is careful lest the entertainment be too harrowing. One no longer becomes poor or rich: both require too much exertion. Who still wants to rule? Who obey? Both require too much exertion. No shepherd and one herd! Everybody wants the same, everybody is the same. . . . "Formerly, all the world was mad," say the most refined, and they blink. . . . One has one's little pleasure for the day and a little pleasure for the night, but one has regard for health. "We have invented happiness"—say the last men, and they blink. (Nietzsche, *Thus Spoke Zarathustra*, 17–18)

about flourishing life almost guarantees that deeper meaning will escape us—and that, if we should stumble on it, we wouldn't even know how to recognize it.

Creeping meaninglessness is a private cost of making the nature of the flourishing life a mere matter of taste. There is public cost as well: cultural "dialogue" about the meaning of human life and about the corresponding "tables of value" ends up looking like the shouting talking heads of cable news. We are unable to reason with—or even speak with—one another about this most important project of our lives, let alone formulate a vision of flourishing life that encompasses all of humanity and all creatures, a pressing concern in a highly interconnected and interdependent world. As a result, many prefer the disengaged individualism of lives built on unreflective soft relativism (your vision is true for you, my vision is true for me) to lives invested in the truth of our common humanity but bereft of any responsible means of contending for it or forging a common bond to it.[34]

Neglected Quest

What truly flourishing life is and how to achieve it is the most important human question. For centuries, it was at the center of great religions and philosophies. Modern ways of living both free us to live as we see fit and place pressure on us to answer always afresh for ourselves what kind of life is worth living. These same modern ways of living, however, undermine our drive and ability to consider in a serious way the question of flourishing life. This is a quick summary of the gray picture we have painted so far. To

34. Martha Nussbaum's summary of humanity's collective plight very much resonates with our own: "If the real clash of civilizations is, as I believe, a clash within the individual soul, as greed and narcissism contend against respect and love, all modern societies are rapidly losing the battle, as they feed the forces that lead to violence and dehumanization and fail to feed the forces that lead to cultures of equity and respect." Martha Nussbaum, *Not for Profit: Why Democracy Needs the Humanities* (Princeton: Princeton University Press, 2012), 143.

complete it, we need to add two dark lines. Two institutions we would expect to educate us in critically exploring and answering this question no longer seem to be taking it seriously.

Universities and the Meaning of Life

One might think that colleges and universities would be the places for sober explorations of the nature of flourishing life, pushing against the deadening effect of the work-and-fun loop we don't know how to escape. Perhaps in an early season of their lives, young people would learn to think intelligently and critically not merely about how to succeed in one or another of their endeavors, but about how to "succeed" in the endeavor that is their life itself. After all, from its beginnings, whether we trace these to Socrates or to the founding of modern universities in the Middle Ages, and throughout most of its history up to the mid-twentieth century, higher education has centered on the question of the meaningful life, true life. The American idea of "college" was invented more or less precisely as a space in which one could ask and answer the big questions of life.[35]

But the great invention has lost much of its original purpose. Our colleges and universities have largely "given up on the meaning of life," to use the phrase that occurs in the subtitle of Anthony Kronman's book about higher education, *Education's End*.[36] Incremental increase in knowledge of the world and in the advances of technological know-how are valued over truth-seeking explorations of meaning and purpose. Especially in an age in which education needs to justify itself in economic terms, whatever accounts are offered of "the value of education" center on instrumental reason and technical skill, not on the goals of human life as a whole and ways to achieve them—not on the character of a life worthy of being called human. Even courses that are about

35. Andrew Delbanco, *College: What It Was, Is, and Should Be* (Princeton: Princeton University Press, 2014), 1, 34.

36. Anthony Kronman, *Education's End: Why Our Colleges and Universities Have Given Up on the Meaning of Life* (New Haven: Yale University Press, 2007).

life, like Stanford's Design Your Life or Yale's Psychology and the Good Life, are more about helping students live the kind of life they want than about discerning the kind of life that is worth wanting. In sum, our educational institutions serve primarily to equip students with skills to be able to generate resources for any kind of life they may decide they want to live.

Churches and the True Life

If we can no longer count on colleges and universities for help in exploring the flourishing life, one might think that religious communities—churches, synagogues, mosques, and temples—would center their activities and explorations on this question. We are not qualified to speak for religions other than Christianity, so we'll limit ourselves to discussing what happens in ecclesial communities. Churches often take up this question—witness the popularity of Rick Warren's *The Purpose-Driven Life*.[37] But it is increasingly common to employ the Christian faith primarily as a set of "skills"—resources!—to manage a life whose course is preset by the demands of success in education and work and by cultural habits formed around leisure and entertainment.

In our private lives, we have a morning coffee, exercise a bit and stretch, and, if we are pious, we have a moment for a devotional reading from the Bible or Oswald Chambers, and off we go to do things whose place in the flourishing life we have never considered in light of our professed faith. Sunday worship services are too frequently no more than a communal version of such energy-boosting, performance-enhancing, or get-well morning exercises. Many churches, of course, do much better, and to the extent they do, they are important schools of the flourishing life.

In two traditional sites of sustained reflection on the flourishing life—the institutions of higher learning and the houses of worship—interest in exploration of the most important question

37. Rick Warren's *The Purpose-Driven Life* (Grand Rapids: Zondervan, 2002) has sold more than thirty million copies and is the second-most-translated book in the world after the Bible.

of human existence is waning. This in itself constitutes a cultural crisis of major proportions, partly because it underpins or exacerbates many other crises. Many have sensed the resulting cultural vacuum and attempted to fill it. Important philosophers have taken up the issue of the "true life," sometimes with the goal of rescuing it from religious captivity and bringing it back to philosophy and to the center of university concerns.[38] Psychologists have done the same, especially those associated with positive psychology,[39] though often with a problematic conflation of scientific knowledge and moral judgment.[40] Religious thinkers from diverse religious traditions wrestle with the issue as well, of course, though often with little awareness of the changed conditions under which the question of flourishing life presents itself to people today. But all this is bucking the trend. Much work remains to reverse it.

A Challenge for Theology

We need to revive a sustained truth-seeking cultural conversation about the flourishing life. We live in a globalized world where partly overlapping and partly contradictory visions of flourishing life coexist in the same public space. People of many diverse perspectives, religious and nonreligious, will need to participate in that conversation. Christian theology ought to become one such voice. If it does, it may be able to help both religious and educational institutions to make the true life their central concern.

Along with philosophy in its ancient mode, for centuries Christian theology served the West as the intellectual space for articulating visions of the flourishing life and sorting out contested

38. Michel Foucault, *The Order of Things: An Archaeology of the Human Sciences* (New York: Random House, 1970); Dworkin, *Religion without God*; Kronman, *Education's End*; Nussbaum, *Not for Profit*.

39. Martin E. P. Seligman and Mihaly Csikszentmihalyi, "Positive Psychology: An Introduction," *American Psychologist* 55, no. 1 (2000): 5–14.

40. See Tamsin Shaw, "The Psychologists Take Power," *New York Review of Books*, February 25, 2016, http://www.nybooks.com/articles/2016/02/25/the -psychologists-take-power.

questions of value. The great church father Augustine placed the problem of the "happy life" at the heart of his theology.[41] In one way or another, all great theologians did the same. With conceptualities appropriate to their contexts, they echoed the orientation of the Christian faith itself toward "the kingdom of God," "life abundant," "new creation," "seeing God," the "new Jerusalem," or—as we argue in chapter 3—toward the establishment of "God's home among humans." Today, too, theology has an indispensable contribution to make in countering taste-driven, individualized, unreflective ways of living and helping people articulate, embrace, and pursue a compelling vision of flourishing life for themselves and all creation.

Theology has a contribution to make, and theology *must make* that contribution if it is to remain true to its purpose, which is the same as the goal of Jesus's mission. One way to see this mission is to look at what Jesus rejected during his temptations immediately before embarking on his mission. The first temptation was the most fundamental. "Turn these stones into bread," the tempter taunted Jesus, who was famished after a forty-day fast in the wilderness. Jesus resisted, responding,

> One does not live by bread alone,
> > but by every word that comes from the mouth of God.
> (Matt. 4:4)

41. Soon after converting, Augustine penned *The Happy Life* (in *"The Happy Life," "Answer to Skeptics," "Divine Providence and the Problem of Evil," "Soliloquies,"* The Fathers of the Church 5, ed. Ludwig Schopp [1948; Washington, DC: Catholic University of America Press, 2010]). As Gareth Matthews notes, the topic is a key concern through the rest of Augustine's career. See especially Augustine, *Confessions*, trans. Henry Chadwick (Oxford: Oxford University Press, 1991), 10.20–23; Augustine, *The City of God*, books 11–22, trans. William Babcock, in *Works of Saint Augustine* I/7 (Hyde Park, NY: New City Press, 2013), 19.1–11; Gareth Matthews, "Happiness," in *Augustine* (Malden, MA: Blackwell, 2005), 134. See also John Bussanich, "Happiness, Eudaimonism," in *Augustine through the Ages*, ed. Allan Fitzgerald (Grand Rapids: Eerdmans, 1999), 413–14; Ragnar Holte, "La béatitude et le Bien suprême," *Béatitude et sagesse: saint Augustin et le problème de la fin de l'homme dans la philosophie ancienne* (Paris: Études augustinennes, 1962), 207–20.

Jesus is quoting the Hebrew Bible here. These words came first to the children of Israel as a summary of the main lesson they were to have learned in the course of their forty years of wandering in the wilderness before entering the promised land. Bread was what they needed in the wilderness. That much was never in doubt; that truth, as insistent as a growling stomach, they didn't need to learn. But they needed more than "bread," and that truth, not as obvious as physical hunger but as real as the possibility of missing their human purpose, they did need to learn. All humans do, perhaps especially we moderns. We have made our greatest temptation into the chief goal of our lives and the main purpose of our major institutions: to create and enjoy ever more sophisticated varieties of "bread."[42]

Living by bread alone, we fail our humanity. When our theology does not provide us with a compelling alternative vision of the good life, it betrays its purpose. This is the tragedy of academic theology today: at the moment when theology's tools are most needed to answer the most pressing question of our lives and to serve the common good, they are found stacked in a corner, dusty and neglected—even or especially by those charged with keeping them sharp. Theology is in crisis, largely because it has lost its nerve and forgotten its purpose to help discern, articulate, and commend compelling visions of flourishing life in light of God's self-revelation in Jesus Christ.

---

42. See Miroslav Volf, "What Will Save the World? Caring for the World We Cannot Save," in *A Calling to Care*, ed. T. W. Herrman (Abilene, TX: Abilene Christian University Press, forthcoming).

2

The Crisis of Theology

Let us be clear from the outset about two things. First, we are talking here about the Western type of Christian academic theology—the kind done in institutions of higher learning and subject to the standards of evaluation accepted by professional guilds and accrediting organizations. We are not talking about Christian theology more generally. It may be that, for instance, "accidental theology" is doing better than academic theology.[1] And it may be that academic theology is flourishing in other parts of the world (for instance, in China or in sub-Saharan Africa).

Second, we use the term "theology" broadly as including all disciplines in the traditional theological faculty from biblical studies to church history and from ethics to ministerial arts; we don't limit the term to systematic theology. Many today do not recognize all these disciplines as "theology"; historians in theological faculties, in particular, often resist being described as theologians.[2] In a way,

---

1. For "accidental theologians," see chap. 1 of this volume.
2. As we see it, not every historian *is* a theologian; but none is not a theologian simply because they are a historian. The two terms need not be mutually exclusive, though they are often experienced as such. Notwithstanding the protestations

we share their sensibility: not all work that happens at a divinity school or a seminary is, or even should be, theological; historians (or sociologists, for that matter) are important to theology *as* historians and sociologists, and they may find their professional home at a theological institution. At the same time, work in all traditional theological disciplines can, and much of it should, be theological. The contestation of this second claim is, we think, part of the crisis of academic theology.

The crisis of theology has two aspects, external and internal. The external crisis is more familiar, though the internal crisis is by far the more significant. We'll begin with the external. To be clear, much of the external crisis is just that: a result of external social, economic, and cultural shifts. But these external pressures expose the *internal* state of theology, which is not healthy in itself. And some of this internal disordering feeds external factors, driving the feedback loops of theology's self-marginalization. We are most familiar with trends in the US and will base our comments on the situation in the US. While important differences exist between American and other late modern contexts, many of the dynamics we describe are features of modern Western societies in general, so we suppose that much of what we say describes the plight of theology in other such contexts as well.

--- **The External Crisis** ---

Shrinking Job Market

When two or more young theologians are gathered these days, they are just as likely to talk about job scarcity and inadequate compensation as about God, God's relation to the world, or the

---

of some historians, we use the word "theology" to refer also to a mode of doing church history; similarly, for us a "young theologian" might well be a scholar of intertestamental literature, despite her Society of Biblical Literature membership. It is "theology" understood in this broadest sense that is in crisis, in part because of its disciplinary disunity.

world's relation to God. This may constitute a failure to live into their theological vocation, but one can understand why: they need to survive and pay off debts in the face of a rapidly shrinking job market.

The job market for academic theologians is closely related to the job market for academically trained ministers. Most mainline denominations still require academic training of their ordinands. But such denominations are a dwindling category with declining congregations, and they are bereft of financial means to actually hire seminary-trained ministers. Many vibrant and growing churches, on the other hand, don't see themselves as needing academically trained ministers.[3] They find theologians and the education they offer at best useless and at worst harmful.[4] Many large local churches train ministers internally in diocesan schools, church-based training programs, or simply through apprenticeship.[5] Such training programs do occasionally employ theologians with advanced academic degrees but not those with the interests and types of training prevalent today in academic institutions or favored by the relevant professional guilds.

Lack of employment opportunities for academically trained clergy puts traditional seminaries and schools of theology themselves in a crisis.[6] After lagging behind general population growth

3. "The churches that have traditionally required a seminary degree are by and large the same denominations whose membership is rapidly declining." Justo L. González, *The History of Theological Education* (Nashville: Abingdon, 2015), x.

4. One might take as anecdotal evidence the old evangelical saw that "seminary" is properly pronounced "cemetery"; it's where faith goes to die.

5. The Lilly Endowment's Insights into Religion remarks that "seminaries are challenged by megachurches that often don't send ministers or lay leaders to seminary, and instead create professional education programs to meet their staffs' needs, . . . [or] have started their own seminaries" ("Theological Education Rebounds, but Fewer Students Enroll," http://www.religioninsights.org/articles /theological-education-rebounds-fewer-students-enroll). The issue isn't exclusively a matter of megachurches; many of the fastest-growing denominations in the past thirty years do not require formal theological education of their clergy.

6. A number of voices are concerned about the current state and trajectory of seminaries. Stanley Hauerwas's concern is so great that on the occasion of speaking at the centennial of Bethany Theological Seminary, he delivered a talk titled "Seminaries Are in Trouble." See appendix B in Stanley Hauerwas, *The State*

for several decades, in recent years seminary enrollment has begun contracting year-over-year.[7] For independent seminaries without the luxury of financial endowments, the drop in enrollment means a financial crisis.[8] Many self-standing seminaries, especially those associated with mainline Protestant denominations, are either closing down or reinventing themselves as nonresidential, online institutions. This means that these institutions hire fewer faculty, and when they do, they often hire adjuncts for minimal pay— certainly below living wages, unless an adjunct is willing and able to teach ten or more courses per year.[9] The expertise of theologians with ten years of advanced degrees can be purchased at a bargain.[10]

of the University: Academic Knowledges and the Knowledge of God (Malden, MA: Blackwell, 2007), 206–8.

7. After experiencing a sudden surge in enrollment in the 1970s, American Theological Society member schools saw enrollment growth that trailed US population growth as a whole in the 1980s and 1990s, a trend made more worrisome when combined with the fact that the enrollment numbers include a growing percentage of part-time students, whose longer periods of study compared to full-time students inflate enrollment numbers. These institutions reported sequential *decreases* in enrollment in reporting periods 2006–2010 and 2010–2014. From 2006 to 2010, institutions reported a 5.6 percent decrease in enrollment; from 2010 to 2014, they reported a 4.9 percent decrease. See American Theological Society, "2010–2011 Annual Data Tables," https://www.ats.edu/upload s/resources/institutional-data/annual-data-tables/2010-2011-annual-data-tables .pdf; American Theological Society, "2014–2015 Annual Data Tables," https:// www.ats.edu/uploads/resources/institutional-data/annual-data-tables/2014-2015 -annual-data-tables.pdf.

8. *Inside Higher Ed* seized on the occasion of Luther Seminary's 2013 layoffs of 18 of its 125 staff members and nonreplacement of 8 of its 44 faculty members as an opportunity to review the dire financial state of American independent seminaries. Libby A. Nelson, "The Struggling Seminaries," *Inside Higher Ed*, March, 29, 2013, https://www.insidehighered.com/news/2013/03/29/luther-seminary-makes -deep-cuts-faculty-and-staff-amid-tough-times-theological. See also G. Jeffrey MacDonald, "Seminaries Face Financial Woes," *USA Today*, March 17, 2009, http://usatoday30.usatoday.com/news/religion/2009-03-17-seminaries_N.htm.

9. To be clear, theological schools are actually better than their nontheological peers in higher education when it comes to adjunct hiring rates, though the problem is still substantial and acutely felt by those caught on the adjunct treadmill.

10. The average annual salary for assistant professors is $56,340 (see table 3.3 of the ATS Annual Data Tables for 2014–15: http://www.ats.edu/uploads/resources /institutional-data/annual-data-tables/2014-2015-annual-data-tables.pdf)—and

Prospects for a job aren't much better in colleges and universities than they are in denominational or independent seminaries. In general, those with PhDs in the humanities are facing a tough job market.[11] Academic theologians share in their economic plight—and in their intellectual plight, as we will argue in what follows. The number of Christianly inflected colleges is shrinking, and even those maintaining a Christian profile are under pressure to reduce the number of requirements in Christian theology broadly construed, often to make room for courses on other religions and relations among religions.[12] For all three reasons mentioned—diminishing demand of churches for academically trained clergy, closing down of seminaries or their transformation into online educational institutions, and loss of interest in theology in universities and colleges—the job market for PhDs in various theological disciplines is shrinking.

Shrinking Audience

Theologians aren't just having a hard time getting hired; those lucky enough to find employment are increasingly losing *audience*. Communities of Christian conviction were theologians' traditional audience, at least the audience for popularized versions of academic theology, as exemplified in the 1950s when popular books by theologians were read widely, for instance, Paul Tillich's immensely

---

these are the lucky folks who are able to secure tenure-track jobs. In the case of adjuncts (who are a growing portion of the population), the undervaluing of theological expertise is especially clear, with effective hourly rates (including preparation time, grading, office hours, and so on) well below $20 per hour.

11. According to a National Science Foundation report, in 2011 just 57 percent of new humanities PhDs had a "definite commitment for employment or postdoctoral study," which is well below the average of 66 percent for all fields—which was itself a low number compared to previous years (https://www.nsf.gov/statistics/2018/nsf18304/data/tab42.pdf).

12. For the history of Christianly inflected colleges and the forces that drive these schools to remove such inflection from their institutional identities, see George Marsden, *The Soul of the American University* (New York: Oxford University Press, 1994). For a discussion of the same trends pertaining to newcomers among Christian colleges, broken down by denomination, see James Burtchaell, *The Dying of the Light: The Disengagement of Colleges and Universities from Their Christian Churches* (Grand Rapids: Eerdmans, 1998).

popular *The Courage to Be*.[13] Today, the number of people in the pew reading academic theology is negligible. The reasons are many. Some of them have to do with the economics of publishing and the technology of knowledge dissemination.[14] Others are related to changes in reading habits more generally or to the widening gap between general-level literacy and the advances of knowledge in distinct subfields—experienced throughout the academy as a difficulty in communicating the significance of scholarly findings to wider audiences. But theologians' loss of audience also largely has to do with the nature of academic theology itself, a topic to which we will return. We note here the loss of interest in theology among communities of faith simply as one indicator of the crisis.

Perhaps laypeople have never read much theology; not many of Augustine's, Thomas Aquinas's, Friedrich Schleiermacher's, or Rudolf Bultmann's lay contemporaries are likely to have read *On the Trinity*, *Summa Theologiae*, *The Christian Faith*, or *Theology of the New Testament*. Over the centuries, however, one small segment of communities of faith—the clergy—used to read the work of academic theologians, both the more technical work and its popular versions. They no longer do, considering it largely irrelevant for their profession.[15] Certainly, changes in the nature of

13. As evidence of the book's impact and broad readership, *The Courage to Be* was included on the New York Public Library's "Books of the Century" list in 1995. As evidence of the decline of theology since then, *The Courage to Be* (1952) was the most recently published theological work on the list; the four more recent publications in the "Mind and Spirit" category were penned by a novelist (Ken Kesey, *One Flew over the Cuckoo's Nest*, 1962), a psychologist (Timothy Leary, *The Politics of Ecstasy*, 1968), a psychiatrist (Elisabeth Kübler-Ross, *On Death and Dying*, 1969), and a psychoanalyst (Bruno Bettelheim, *The Uses of Enchantment*, 1976). Elizabeth Diefendorf, *The New York Public Library's Books of the Century* (New York: Oxford University Press, 1997).

14. Books are increasingly written and sold for predetermined audiences; publishers engage in targeted marketing and don't pursue a larger readership if they know they can make money from a particular audience. The policy of "no-books-without-significant-following" hinders the engagement of theologians with wider audiences.

15. As part of a 2001–2005 national study of pastors in the US, Jackson Carroll and Becky McMillan asked pastors to list the three authors they most often read in relation to their work as pastors. Carroll and McMillan put together top-ten

the profession are part of the reason for this. The era of "learned clergy" seems to be past. Many ministers are more the church's institutional managers than its theological guides; correspondingly, many read more management ("leadership") books than they do works of academic theology. Reflecting the sensibilities and interests of their parishioners, ministers are often more likely to consult a book in pop psychology or pop social critique than a treatise in theology.

Academic theologians, on their part, return the favor—or perhaps it is they who are above all driving the unhappy exchange. With notable exceptions (including many in practical theology), we academic theologians consider neither laypeople nor clergy relevant to our work: we research and write neither for them nor with them in view, but rather for the guild and for the tenure review committees at the institutions where we teach. In seminaries and divinity schools—institutions that function as professional schools—we theologians are often hesitant to receive input from clergy about our teaching, let alone about our research. The result? We have little to say to the clergy.

Having lost its traditional audience, has academic theology acquired a new one? It has not. The wider public outside Christian communities perceives academic theology as so thoroughly irrelevant that it might as well not exist. The main exceptions are popular publications of scholars who seek to show that one or the other of traditional Christian convictions—about what Jesus did or said, for instance—is untrue.[16] To introduce yourself as a

---

lists from each of the four denominational traditions the survey tracked. Of the twenty-seven unique individuals included across these four lists, only *six* were academic theologians. Jackson W. Carroll, *God's Potters: Pastoral Leadership and the Shaping of Congregations* (Grand Rapids: Eerdmans, 2006), 109.

16. E.g., Bart Ehrman's works: *Forged: Writing in the Name of God—Why the Bible's Authors Are Not Who We Think They Are* (New York: HarperCollins, 2011); *Misquoting Jesus: The Story behind Who Changed the Bible and Why* (New York: HarperCollins, 2005); *The Orthodox Corruption of Scripture: The Effect of Early Christological Controversies on the Text of the New Testament* (New York: Oxford University Press, 1993); *God's Problem: How the Bible Fails to Answer Our Most Important Question—Why We Suffer* (New York: HarperOne, 2008).

theologian at a party or during a flight often elicits puzzled stares, not wide-open eyes. The common perception is that theology isn't offering anything useful.

The loss of audience for academic theology is also visible in the shrinking market for theological books (though, of course, a shift in the character of the means of communication has much to do with the matter as well). Two examples may suffice. In the nineteenth and through most of the twentieth century, Germany was the center of theological thinking. Today, its population of 80 million will purchase almost no theological books. The most prominent professors at the most prestigious universities write books that are often printed in no more than 500 copies, and most of these go to universities, mainly for their libraries. In the English-speaking world—presently the cultural space in which most theological books are produced—even with 360 million native speakers and with English as the lingua franca of the world and the main language of the sciences, a book by an academic theologian from a prestigious university might have an initial printing of 1,500 copies and never have a second printing. Some theologians are more widely read, but, as Amazon rankings indicate, they are the exception rather than the rule.

The issue isn't simply that theologians aren't making their work *accessible*. Popularizing the latest findings of their discipline—something scholars in all disciplines, from physics to psychology, strive to do—won't help theologians unless they can make plain to the public that what they have to say matters. There is no gain in communicating eloquently and accessibly what has already been deemed arcane and vacuous. Some invoke increased secularization in the West to explain diminished interest in the work of academic theologians. But that won't do. After all, secularization has not advanced much in the last half century, certainly not nearly as much as was predicted or as would be needed to explain the widespread disinterest in academic theology.[17] People simply no longer look

17. Elizabeth Shakman Hurd, *The Politics of Secularism and International Relations* (Princeton: Princeton University Press, 2008), 134–54.

for answers to life's big questions in theological books. If these questions are posed or answered anywhere, it may be in popular psychology and self-help manuals. Granted, Christian theology now has many more competitors than it did half a century ago: all manner of intellectuals—psychologists, cognitive scientists, biologists, legal scholars—as well as motivational speakers from religious or nonreligious backgrounds. No doubt, competitors have partly squeezed theology out of its public role. But intentionally or unintentionally, theologians have also ceded ground to competitors in a failed attempt to regain academic respectability. We will return to this point in a moment.

Are academic theologians, then, the audience of academic theology? One would think so. But even that might be too much to say—if by academic theologians we mean, as we do, a broad range of scholars who teach and research in theological schools. Subdivided as theology is into specialized fields, its audiences tend to be subfield-specific, often limited only to those working within a narrow slice of a subfield. Biblical scholars working in different subfields don't necessarily read one another's work. And many systematic theologians have read more scholarly work on Karl Marx, Friedrich Nietzsche, Jacques Derrida, Judith Butler, or whoever else the currently popular intellectual might be, than they have read scholarly work of their colleagues on the Gospel of John or the letters of Paul—let alone on Isaiah or Amos.

Shrinking Reputation

Finally, theology has suffered a substantial *loss of intellectual reputation* within the academy and beyond its walls. Indeed, scholars in other academic disciplines are part of the wider public indifference to theology. That's not just because, more generally, scholars in distinct disciplines don't read one another's work. Much more troubling, theology has lost their esteem. While he was president of Harvard University, Larry Summers told one of us that were Harvard University to be founded today, it wouldn't have a divinity school. He made the remark in passing, as if it didn't need any explanation or elaboration; worse, he made it in the context of a search for the dean of Harvard's divinity school. What Summers put bluntly, others—university professors no less than university administrators—often think but don't bother to articulate. The general sense is that theology isn't producing any genuine knowledge that accomplishes anything, that it trades with the irrationality of faith and is useless.[18] Theology was among the founding disciplines of modern universities, the queen of sciences. Today, in many universities and colleges the queen has been deposed; in others she has been tucked away at the very edge of her erstwhile domain out of institutional inertia and, perhaps, a bit of respect for her bygone power and renown.

Various pieces of this crisis work together to reinforce one another and deepen theology's marginalization. The shrinking job market makes job security in the form of tenure the top priority, meaning that publication, for aspiring theologians, becomes a matter of professional credentialing. The academic presses acknowledge this and therefore begin to operate precisely this way—that is, as credentialing institutions rather than as publishing houses, with little effort applied to helping theologians find an audience. Ironically, the loss of intellectual reputation drives theologians to double down on seeking professional validation within the academy, further alienating them from potential audiences in the church and the broader culture. The shrinking job market and loss of audience reinforce each other: academic theologians teach fewer people to be interested in what they are doing, so fewer and fewer people read and appreciate what they write. As a result, academic institutions hire fewer theologians who teach fewer students, and the cycle of theologians' marginalization continues.

To exaggerate a bit: academic theology today is composed of specialists in an unrespected discipline who write for fellow

18. Some of the perceived irrelevance of theology comes from the sense that it isn't producing any *genuine* knowledge (the problem of theology's perceived irrationality), and, given the dominance of instrumental rationality in modernity and therefore in today's universities, some of it comes from the sense that theology isn't producing any *useful* knowledge (the problem of theology's perceived disutility).

specialists about topics that interest hardly anyone else. Perhaps that is as it must be and perhaps that is even as it should be—the fate of a "soft" academic discipline in an age of exponential growth in specialized knowledge and the fate of a discipline that studies religion in a pragmatic age of astounding increases in ability to manipulate the world for human benefit. There is something to this explanation of theology's marginality. Theology has no spectacular new insights to offer, nothing analogous to information about mountain ranges on dwarf planet Pluto or the genetic basis of certain cancers; there are no stunning new tools to whose design theology has contributed, nothing analogous to a driverless car or the material magic of graphene. What *does* theology have to offer? The external crisis of theology—loss of jobs, loss of audience, loss of reputation—has much to do with the stuttering of theologians as they try to answer this question. Its external crisis, that is, stems in part from an internal crisis.

The Internal Crisis

Academic theology could weather its external crisis were it not for a serious illness that affects its own body. Theology is a vocation; as such, it does not depend on external validation and, from time to time, may well involve persisting in the face of resistance and seeming irrelevance. And yet it is hard for theology to persist when it has forgotten its purpose: to critically discern, articulate, and commend visions of the true life in light of the person, life, and teachings of Jesus Christ.[19] This is the one complex illness that afflicts theology today, its most important crisis. The illness has given rise to two destructive coping strategies, which are tied to two central dimensions of theology, descriptive and normative, each as indispensable as the other. The first coping

19. For this purpose of theology see chap. 3 in this volume.

strategy reduces theology to a deficient version of its descriptive dimension; the second reduces it to a deficient version of its normative dimension. While each strategy has natural affinities with particular theological disciplines, both reductions can be found operating within every theological discipline. We'll take each strategy in turn.

Theology as "Science"

The first strategy evolved as a response to the ascendancy of the "research ideal" in universities in the late nineteenth century, which itself was largely an echo of the immense reputation the natural sciences and their methodologies have garnered for themselves as producers of reliable and useful knowledge.[20] In such an intellectual environment, theology could turn into scientific study of religion, and theologians—along with many other humanities scholars—could come to understand themselves as primarily engaged in a knowledge-producing enterprise, in an endeavor to incrementally increase the human grasp of the world.[21] In a typical theological institution of higher learning today, perhaps as many as half the faculty identify themselves as "historians" of one stripe or another—including, as would undoubtedly have shocked their

20. Marsden, *Soul of the American University*, 153; Anthony Kronman, *Education's End: Why Our Colleges and Universities Have Given Up on the Meaning of Life* (New Haven: Yale University Press, 2007), 91–136; Anthony Delbanco, *College: What It Was, Is, and Should Be* (Princeton: Princeton University Press: 2014), 67–101.

21. Friedrich Schleiermacher was among the first to implement this strategy. In *Brief Outline of the Study of Theology as a Field of Study*, he divides theological disciplines and frames as many as possible in descriptive terms, as historical disciplines. Under the heading "Historical Theology," he lists not only "exegetical theology," "historical theology in the narrower sense," and "church history"—disciplines we would be inclined to call "historical"—but also "the historical Knowledge of the Present Condition of Christianity." Even dogmatic theology becomes a descriptive discipline, the natural partner of "ecclesiastical statistics." Only "philosophical theology" and "practical theology" are excluded from the domain of "historical theology." Friedrich Schleiermacher, *Brief Outline of the Study of Theology as a Field of Study*, trans. Terrence Tice, 3rd ed. (Louisville: Westminster John Knox, 2011), §§69–256, pp. 31–69.

premodern predecessors, nearly all biblical scholars.[22] Even some who don't, like practical theologians, increasingly see themselves as social scientists. We'll call this current distortion of theology's descriptive dimension "theology as science," with "science" here being understood in the modern sense.

For theology as science, the subject matter of theology is *Christianity*, or more broadly the world of religions, rather than, as traditionally understood, God and everything else in relation to God (Thomas Aquinas) or "the knowledge of God and ourselves" (Martin Luther and John Calvin), or, as we will argue shortly, the world as the home of God ("the kingdom of God," in the terminology of the Gospels).[23] A shift in the self-understanding of theology occurred—away from God or from God-and-the-world-in-relation and toward a particular segment of the world (Christianity or religions in general), and away from norms and purposes and toward facts and causes.[24]

Let us be clear: knowledge and understanding of Christianity always was and must remain a crucial *part* of theological endeavors. The dynamic and changing world of Christianity—its abiding roots in the story and sacred texts of the people of Israel and emergence from Judaism in the context of Greco-Roman antiquity, its spread over time and transmission to diverse cultures, its present shape and function under a variety of circumstances, the inner logic of its convictions, and its potential future—all this needs to

22. The preponderance of "historical identities" can be deduced at the national level by considering the more or less equal membership of the Society of Biblical Literature (8,500 members) and the American Academy of Religion (9,500 members), assuming that most if not all SBL members would be willing—in one way or another—to own the title "historian" and that a large minority of the members of AAR would also accept this title.

23. See chap. 3 in this volume. For the classical description of the subject matter of theology see Thomas Aquinas, *Summa Theologiae* I.1.7.

24. The strength of the shift is evident in the fact that "causes" and "purposes" are now two mutually exclusive categories (except, maybe, in the case of "fighting for the cause"), while in the Aristotelian schema a purpose is precisely one type of cause (*telos* is a kind of *aitia*): see Aristotle, *Metaphysics*, books 1–9, trans. Hugh Tredennick, Loeb Classical Library, ed. T. E. Page, E. Capps, and W. H. D. Rouse (London: Heinemann, 1933), 1013a–b, pp. 208–15.

be studied and understood adequately with help from relevant disciplines: history, philology, sociology, psychology, study of religion, and so on. This immense intellectual undertaking requires hard-nosed research that furnishes genuine and useful knowledge. It is not just that without such research we would remain in the dark about a religion that encompasses 2.3 billion people. Were it to abandon such research, theology's very methodology would distort the Christian faith as it would tacitly "excarnate" a religion that has at its core an event of incarnation. But were theology to limit itself to such research, were it to proceed as if it were another science, it would fail in its very methodology to sufficiently honor the goal of the incarnation, which is to help align the world with God's purposes.

When theology sees itself as a science in this sense, three significant consequences follow. First, as we have noted earlier, incremental increase in knowledge is gained today through progressive disciplinary specialization, and this specialization often means loss of the sense of the unity of the subject matter studied. The name of our institutions of higher learning—"university"—suggests that scholars working in them are pursuing knowledge that fits into a unified whole, and, indeed, theology used to function precisely as the unifying science. Yet apart from some interdisciplinary teaching, today's universities are largely a collection of discrete research centers, mostly working within a single discipline.[25] They produce staggering amounts of data and useful insights, but these tend to be splintered rather than unified; the university produces "knowledges," as it is sometimes expressed, but not knowledge.[26] The same is true of theology when its sole purpose is the incremental increase in knowledge. We academic theologians then generate

25. Clark Kerr, the former president of the University of California system who coined the term "multiversity," famously joked that the university has become merely "a series of individual faculty entrepreneurs held together by a common grievance over parking." Clark Kerr, *The Uses of the University* (Cambridge, MA: Harvard University Press), 15.

26. See Hauerwas, *State of the University: Academic Knowledges and the Knowledge of God.*

immense amounts of interesting research, but sometimes we don't know and too often we don't care how individual bits and pieces of theological "data" add up to a unity, let alone how they all figure in an articulation of a coherent way of life. For some disciplines, absence of unity may not present a problem. For theology it does.

This lack of unity feeds into the second problem with the reduction of theology to knowledge acquisition: an inability to address normative questions. As scientists, theologians can talk about what is and what is likely to be, but not about what should be and what we ought to hope for in the future. This, too, is a fate theology shares with humanistic disciplines, which have also traded their ability to address the "big questions" of human life for academic respectability in an intellectual environment dominated by the sciences.[27] Denied both their traditional home in theology and their newer nineteenth-century humanistic domicile, the big questions of life are now more or less absent from the academy entirely.[28] Such questions were traditionally the central, though never the only, dimension of theological endeavor.[29] Theologians

27. Paula M. Cooey, "The Place of Academic Theology in the Study of Religion from the Perspective of Liberal Education," in *Religious Studies, Theology, and the University: Conflicting Maps, Changing Terrain*, ed. Linell E. Cady and Delwin Brown (Albany: SUNY Press, 2002), 179.

28. In invoking a new humanistic domicile for the big questions, we mean to refer to a period of time during which, in theology's absence, the big questions of life were doggedly pursued in a secular humanist mode. Kronman, *Education's End*, 74–90.

29. Commenting on the phrase "expectation of creation" from Rom. 8, Martin Luther distanced himself from the way philosophers and metaphysicians of his time talked about creation, addressing only the question of "what now is" and failing to attend to "that which is still in the future." He compared them to "a man who, joining himself to a builder and marveling at the cutting and hewing and measuring of the wood and the beams, is foolishly content and quiet among these things, without concern as to what the builder finally intends to make by all of these exertions." Luther's philosophers and metaphysicians thematize only the "mechanics" of the world but not its final end. And since the world is in the grip of suffering, they "derive a happy science out of a sad creation." Martin Luther, *Lectures on Romans*, in *Luther's Works* (St. Louis: Concordia, 1972), 25:361–62. It is fundamental to the work of theologians, he believed, not only to describe the past and the present, but also to speak normatively about the future, to articulate what we may hope for and what we ought to desire.

who see themselves as contributing to the incremental increase in the knowledge and understanding of Christianity feel uneasy in offering practical wisdom, normative judgments, or proposals about Christian convictions and practices. And rightly so, for when we reduce theology to knowledge acquisition, the methodological constraint we operate under leaves little room for practical wisdom and normative judgments.[30] When theologians offer these, we end up doing so as amateurs rather than as scholars—and the quality of what we produce often reflects our status as amateurs.

Third, a focus on increasing our knowledge of the world places the wrong object and wrong purpose of study at the center. This is not an object and purpose of study in which theology has no vital interest *qua* theology but an object and purpose that belong to a different and important discipline (or, more accurately, a set of subdisciplines)—namely, the study of religion.[31] The mission statement of Yale Divinity School, "to foster the knowledge and love of God" (the source, model, and chief end of human beings), articulates succinctly and accurately the classical self-understanding of theology as an academic discipline. But it can easily conflict with the self-understanding of scholars whose main purpose is incrementally increasing their knowledge of Christianity. They can foster knowledge of the *professed* knowledge and love of God and of the *effects* of such knowledge and love of God on individuals and societies, but they cannot foster the knowledge and love of *God* without first taking off their professional mantle. Reducing

30. Of course, it is not as though reducing theology to knowledge acquisition is possible, strictly speaking. All theological work (indeed, all humanistic inquiry) always has normative interests; it makes claims about the nature of the world and our place in it. The modernist reduction of theology to "science" doesn't so much remove normative interests as it conceals them. Its claims to "objectivity," therefore, are disingenuous. (This disingenuousness is not lost on theology's critics within the academy, which feeds the academic existential anxiety that drives theologians' desire to reduce their field to "objective description"; it is a vicious feedback loop.)

31. For ways of construing this vital relationship between theology and the study of religion, see David F. Ford, "Theology and Religious Studies at the Turn of the Millennium: Reconceiving the Field," *Teaching Theology and Religion* 1, no. 1 (1998): 4–12; Cooey, "Place of Academic Theology," 172–86.

the purpose of theology to an incremental increase in knowledge is also incompatible with the amended classical account of theology we propose in this book: the essential core of theological work is critically examining, articulating, and commending a vision of flourishing life inscribed in the story of Jesus Christ, God come to dwell among humans. Theology done in an exclusively descriptive mode misses a key dimension of its purpose—and fails to attend to a central challenge in the contemporary world, namely to discern with intellectual integrity the shape of genuinely flourishing life.

Distortions of Normativity

Reducing theology to "science" is not the only strategy theology has developed to cope with its internal crisis. The constructive disciplines don't want to see themselves as mere producers of scholarly knowledge, and many theologians (ourselves included) have still pursued theology as a normative intellectual endeavor. But their efforts are often barren in content and effect. The issue is not, as the complaint sometimes goes, that theologians like to debate arcane topics that seem detached from real life.[32] That may be the

32. The proverbial question of how many angels can dance on the head of a pin is a caricature, humorous only to those who don't appreciate the discussion because they have not taken the time to understand it. A lot is at stake in such a question for a theologian like Thomas Aquinas, who himself entertained a version of this fabled concern in *questions* like "Whether several angels can be at the same time in the same place?" (*Summa Theologiae* I.52.3). Thomas contends that angels are incorporeal beings having form but no matter, an assertion that branches into some of the most fundamental doctrines of his metaphysics. He must account for how angels can have location without extension. That he does so means that the answer to the question posed above is obvious: there can be a potentially *infinite* number of angels on the head of a pin! This is not just an important metaphysical clarification (though it is certainly that; an angel is, for Thomas, in a place in a different way than a human being is, or than God is). It is also crucial for explaining how angels can be present to us. The "Sed contra" for *Summa Theologiae* I.52.1, "Whether an angel is in a place?," is drawn from the Dominican breviary's service for compline: "*On the contrary,* It is said in the Collect: 'Let Thy holy angels who dwell herein, keep us in peace'"—a prayer that continues to be said by countless Christians across the world today. Thomas's careful reflection on how angels, beings having no matter to speak of, can nonetheless

case, but there are more significant problems for the normative engagements of theologians: nostalgia and attempts at repristination (on the conservative side) and suspicion and unending critique (on the liberal side).

Many theologians in conservative circles clutch nostalgically to past convictions and ways of life, as if the beliefs, practices, and cultural mores of their pious great-grandparents were of heavenly origin. With regard to convictions, they see themselves as engaged in the noble work of shoring up "the faith that was once for all entrusted to the saints" (Jude 3) against the corrosive effects of changed circumstances, altered cultural sensibilities, and new knowledge. In an important sense, we agree with them: it is a necessary and laudable theological task to rearticulate ancient creeds and their scriptural sources in today's world. The reason is simple: the Christian faith rests on a positive revelation, above all on the Word become flesh in Jesus Christ. Yet theology is trivialized when it is reduced to simply rehearsing and doggedly defending past articulations of the faith, as if the same thing needs to be said at every time and in every place or as if the same formulation means the same thing when used at different times and in different places. We also give up on the quest for truth when we marshal all forces—in exegesis and history as well as in philosophical, moral, and practical theology—to "discover" and corroborate predetermined dogmatic stances. To compromise our commitment to the truth in this way is no small thing. In fact, we undo ourselves as Christians and responsible theologians when we do so, and we undermine theology as a reputable academic discipline.

A nostalgic and defensive stance toward past articulations of the faith often goes hand in hand with a similarly "defensive" stance toward past cultural forms. We then hear jeremiads about the demise of Christian values in various domains of life or, more encompassingly, about entire nations' or even continents' loss of Christian character, a practice that feeds on apocalyptic narratives

---

dwell with us is thus only *apparently* irrelevant to the life of discipleship. (Many thanks to Justin Crisp for helping prepare this note.)

of cultural and civilizational decline as well as on the misplaced dominance in post-Reformation theology of the "sin/redemption" axis in understanding faith and doing theology. The issue is not whether or not significant moral losses have occurred in the rapid transformation of largely Christianly inflected cultures; they have occurred, though gains have been made as well. It is rather that time cannot be made to flow backward and that condemnations and calls to repentance, though important, are subsidiary forms of Christian engagement with the broader culture. As Christian theologians, we are not followers of John the Baptist, the prophet of national repentance, but of Jesus Christ, the bringer of the good news to the whole world. The core of our response toward moral decline—where and when it exists—should be to articulate a *positive* vision of life that calls us *forward*.

When it comes to overcoming the crisis of theology, things aren't any better in the *progressive camp* of normatively engaged theologians. For many, Christian convictions have been emptied of truth content; they are, even at their best, moves in a cultural power-game, crafted and employed to achieve certain desirable social ends. Those ends themselves typically turn out to be some variation of the modern triple concern with removing limits to freedom, fighting exclusion, and mitigating suffering. All three of these concerns are central to the Christian faith as well. But by inserting them into an overarching vision of flourishing life for all creatures—God's home in the world, as we will argue shortly— the Christian faith gives them a particular form. Our theology is insufficiently *Christian*—and less revealing of the truth than it should be, if Christian claims are indeed *true* (as we believe them to be)—when we repeat in religious idiom normative stances that nontheologians advocate, often with better arguments and greater rhetorical power.

Now, Christian communities and theologians share both common humanity and moral situations with their non-Christian contemporaries. As a result, the issues they face are often the same, and the proper stance toward them may be the same, or at least similar, as well. There is, therefore, nothing wrong with moral learning from "outsiders"; Paul Tillich, one of the great progressive theologians from the last century, was right to identify and honor the phenomenon of "reverse prophetism."[33] For instance, the churches needed to learn something about the structural causes of poverty in modern societies and therefore to recast the way we think of care of the poor, and to the extent that we have done this, we have done so in great part by learning from non-Christians. This is as it should be. Yet that cannot be all theologians need to say. When one reads some of the work that takes up modern concern for freedom, inclusion, and relief of suffering, it is not always clear what value theologians add, except to help underwrite with religious reasons positions others have already articulated and to help spread them among religious folks. Though producing knock-offs has kept many a company from closing, the endeavor has garnered respect for none of them.

But it isn't just that the moral concerns of many progressive theologians merely echo those of their colleagues in other fields in the humanities. Their approach to those concerns is similar as well. Conservatives like jeremiads; progressives relish critique. They interrogate and unmask; they trouble and problematize; they expose and subvert; they demystify and destabilize.[34] For theologians no less than for nontheologians who practice it, critique is often infinite; it applies to everything—to biblical texts and biblical figures, to the church today and throughout its history, to God and to all aspects of modern societies—and it never stops.

Some of the progressive critical impetus comes from the Christian tradition itself,[35] not just from the prophetic castigation of misuse of political power or religious rituals, but from the conviction that sin is most powerful when it appears as goodness, and

33. Paul Tillich, *Systematic Theology* (Chicago: University of Chicago Press, 1967), 3:214.

34. We draw in this paragraph on Rita Felski, *The Limits of Critique* (Chicago: University of Chicago Press, 2015). See also Elizabeth S. Anker and Rita Felski, eds., *Critique and Postcritique* (Durham, NC: Duke University Press, 2017).

35. See Simon During, "The Eighteenth-Century Origins of Critique," in Anker and Felski, *Critique and Postcritique*, 74–96.

therefore it conspires to present itself as godliness. And yet there is a fundamental difference. Today's critique, as a rule, offers no positive alternative; its normativity is antinormative.[36] Unlike the prophets of old, many theologians today engage not just in criticism but in what some critics of critique have called "critiquiness."[37] They shy away from offering a positive vision in whose service they undertake their critique; for then this vision, too, would recursively become a target of the critique.[38] In the absence of a positive vision, critiques easily devolve to mere griping, knocking things down. Unmasking gives the impression of intellectual profundity, and griping offers the cheap thrill of understated self-righteousness. Both get old quickly and accomplish little; in fact, as the biblical admonition regarding exorcism suggests, they often make things worse (Matt. 12:43–45). To change the world, we need an "I have a dream" speech, not an "I have a complaint" speech. Without daring a positive proposal, this mode of normative theological engagement can neither secure freedom, its most central value, nor identify what counts as exclusion, or even as suffering: all three concerns presuppose a certain kind of stability of identity, a form of closure that critique cannot tolerate.[39]

36. So Felski, *Limits of Critique*, 9. For a sophisticated discussion of normativity and antinormativity in queer theory and theology, see Linn Marie Tonstad, "Ambivalent Loves: Christian Theologies, Queer Theologies," in *Literature & Theology* 31, no. 4 (2017): 472–89.

37. In *Limits of Critique* (87–88) Felski takes up this "inspired coinage" of Christopher Castiglia to describe "an unmistakable blend of suspicion, self-confidence, and indignation" that is the hallmark of this particular mode of critique. See Christopher Castiglia, "Critiquiness," *English Language Notes* 51, no. 2 (2013): 79–85.

38. As it turns out, such engagements, whether on the part of theologians or nontheologians, are in fact always based on a vision of the good. That vision is rarely articulated or defended but merely assumed, however.

39. On the need for certain kind of closure for affirming and securing freedom, see Terry Eagleton, *Ideology: An Introduction* (New York: Verso, 1991), 197–98:

Language itself is infinitely productive; but this incessant productivity can be artificially arrested into "closure"—into the sealed world of ideological stability. . . . The speaking subject "forgets" the discursive formation which sets him in place, so for this mode of thought ideological representation involves repressing the work of language, the material process of signifying

Theology as . . .	Descriptive	Normative	
Science	+	−	Descriptive knowledge, whether historical, philosophical, sociological, etc. E.g., theology as religious studies.
Advocacy	−	+	Something like Hume's "brute moral reactions." E.g., griping against what is condemned or fantasizing aloud about what is commended.
Theology	+	+	*Descriptive work in service of a normative vision of human flourishing.*

Table 2.1 Misconstruals of theology when its descriptive and normative aspects are not held in productive tension. The descriptive and normative modes of theology are both indispensable.

Doing theology as mere critique isn't only inconsistent and ineffectual. The overall effect of this mode of theologizing is to marginalize theology *as* theology in the very act of doing it. How much theology do you need in order to be against curtailing freedom, against exclusion, against suffering? Likely much, if you are interested in a Christianly inflected understanding of freedom, exclusion, suffering, and againstness. None, if you resist all closure and assume that what freedom, exclusion, and suffering *are* is self-evident. Theology reduced to this mode of critique is fundamentally atheological.

---

production which underlies these coherent meanings and can always potentially subvert them. . . . Politically speaking, this is a latently libertarian theory of the subject, which tends to "demonize" the very act of semiotic closure. . . . It occasionally betrays an anarchic suspicion of meaning as such; and it falsely assumes that "closure" is always counterproductive. But such closure is a provisional effect of any semiosis whatsoever, and may be politically enabling rather than constraining; "Reclaim the night!" involves a semiotic and (in one sense of the term) ideological closure, but its political force lies precisely in this. . . . Whether such closure is politically positive or negative depends on the discursive and ideological context. . . . A certain provisional stability of identity is essential not only for psychical well-being but for revolutionary political agency.

When constructive theology's normative engagement has the feel of a knock-off and consists in knock-downs, a nagging suspicion arises that in its normative moral stances, theology isn't concerned with questions of truth and goodness but serves merely as a tool—and, of all tools, primarily as a crowbar, a jackhammer, a demolition ball. Perhaps theology is useful to get a preset demolition job done (and, doubtless, there are demolition jobs that need to be done), but it offers inadequate accounts of why something should be demolished in the first place and is unable to say much substantive about what should replace the demolished edifice.

	As Self-Described	As They Actually Are	As Theology Ought to Be
Conservative	(pure) restatement of faith	unthematized new articulation	thematized (and carefully discerned) new articulation of faith
Progressive	(pure) negation	critique based on unthematized vision of flourishing life	critique based on thematized (and carefully discerned) vision of flourishing life

Table 2.2 Deficient normativities, conservative and progressive

We reject these prevalent modes of normative engagement of both conservative *and* progressive theologians not in order to advocate a disengaged theology. But theology's engagement needs to be both more theological and more transformative. Neither reactionary pining for a nonexistent lost golden age nor progressive griping bereft of positive vision will suffice. The corruption and injustice of our world demand a more theological response. The urgency of these issues—from the mounting deaths of black Americans at the hands of police officers, to the throngs of dislocated and yet unwelcome migrants, to the plight of those laboring in sweatshops under the oppressive hand of unscrupulous profit seekers, to the ever-widening gap between rich and poor—highlights the need for a theology able to articulate visions of truly flourishing life that will intellectually fund transformative political engagement.

────────────── **The Real Value of Theology** ──────────────

In light of theology's deep internal crisis, our frequent complaint that our discipline isn't deemed significant and its practitioners aren't paid well needs to be turned back to us academic theologians: How significant an enterprise is academic theology? Let's slip for a moment into the shoes of an academic administrator (or, for that matter, any responsible citizen of the world or committed follower of Christ) and think in terms of costs and benefits. Let's take first the costs. At a place like Yale, a postgraduate education of a single student through the PhD program has a price tag of close to one million dollars total or about one hundred thousand dollars per year—that's all costs included, whoever is paying them, for education beyond college.[40] And that's just training; that's before you actually pay such expertise to go to work. A full-time academic theologian is on average paid about ninety-three thousand dollars per year, including benefits.[41] That puts the total cost, from postgraduate education through retirement, at roughly four million dollars. What are the benefits? Define them in whatever terms you like: the faith stirred by those who are educated by such minds or inspired by their writings; the unjust social structures toppled because of their scathing political diatribe (should there be any); the value of the incremental increase of the knowledge of Christianity. The internal crisis of theology means that this value is unclear at best. Given the state of academic theology today, why does the world need million-dollar theological heads working for ninety-three thousand dollars a year? Why aren't the ten

40. These figures are a composite of rough estimates of Gregory Sterling, the present dean (2013–) and Harold Attridge, the previous dean (2002–2012).

41. This is the "Average Total Compensation" for all full-time faculty at reporting ATS member institutions (American Theological Society, "2014–2015 Annual Data Tables," table 3.3, http://www.ats.edu/uploads/resources/institutional-data /annual-data-tables/2014-2015-annual-data-tables.pdf). This, of course, does not cover their full cost, which would include shares of support staff and administrator salaries, the cost of libraries and infrastructure, etc., which is why theologians appear cheaper to employ than to train (the rough estimates for the cost of training above include these support and infrastructure costs).

long years of postgraduate study of academic theology followed by thirty working years just a massive waste of time and money?[42] Why should we employ and pay academic theologians—even pay them *poorly* (as we increasingly do)?

There are good answers to these questions, but they all presuppose a transformation in the self-understanding of academic theology. Because what theology *really is for* offers genuine value—and not just for the church, but for the world.

42. Examining whether academic theologians are worth the money they are paid may seem a perverse exercise to some theologians. We generally complain about being underpaid. But unless we can show our benefit, the question whether academic theologians are a waste of resources will inevitably arise, and rightly so. Without a better account of the value that theologians provide, the complaint that theologians are underpaid—and we think they are!—will seem utterly self-interested and unpersuasive.

3

The Renewal of Theology

To counter the crisis of theology and enable theologians to generate and enrich truth-seeking conversations about the most important question of our lives, we need to change the way we do theology. The heart of our proposal concerns the purpose of theology. It is to discern, articulate, and commend visions of and paths to flourishing life in light of the self-revelation of God in the life, death, resurrection, exaltation, and coming in glory of Jesus Christ, with this entire story, its lows and its highs, bearing witness to a truly flourishing life.

The Purpose of Theology

But why make flourishing life the purpose of theology? Simply put, because Christian faith in its entirety is about flourishing life—good life, true life, or, in biblical terms, "abundant life" (John 10:10) or "the life that really is life" (1 Tim. 6:19). Christian theology should follow suit. Flourishing life should be the encompassing purpose that all theologians' endeavors serve.

Varieties of the One Purpose

To make flourishing life the purpose of theology may seem an innovation, but it is not. The term "flourishing life" is not common in the tradition, but the substance to which it refers is everywhere. It is possible to read all the great Christian theologians as offering versions of the Christian account of the flourishing life—Augustine and Maximus the Confessor, Aquinas and Bonaventure and Julian of Norwich, Luther and Calvin, and Schleiermacher, to name only a few of the most remarkable theologians from a more distant past. Some of them, like Augustine, oriented their theology toward the good life explicitly; others, like Luther, did so implicitly but no less decidedly, partly because, living in the largely unified world of Christendom, they were exempt from the pressure always to explicate the Christian vision of the true life against the backdrop of other options (though Luther did articulate the pillar of his vision of the true life, the unconditionality of God's grace, in contrast not just to Catholic and Anabaptist accounts of the good life but also to those of Jews and Muslims). But all of these theologians advocated an integrated vision of flourishing life rooted in the self-revelation of God in Jesus Christ.

Some of the visions associated with these figures differ enough from one another to function as *rival* versions, even though each is Christianly plausible. Even within a single version, there is variation, as the varieties of Thomism or Lutheranism illustrate; a single version of the Christian vision of the flourishing life may house multiple varieties of that life. Temperamental predilections and contextual heterogeneity often play a role—differences in geography, in available technologies, in social organization of life, in surrounding religious and broader cultural landscapes, and so on.[1] In some ways, the flourishing life comes in as many versions

1. Varieties of the flourishing life can be divided into categories, of course. Early on, for instance, Christian theologians recognized two basic varieties of the flourishing life, exemplified by two sisters, Martha and Mary, who were friends of Jesus (Luke 10:38–42) and who came to stand for the *vita activa* and *vita contemplativa*, respectively. Especially since the Reformation, Christian theologians have

as there are human beings. Though none of us flourishes alone, each of us flourishes—or not—in our own unique way.

Differences in accounts of the flourishing life have not been first introduced into Christian faith by postbiblical generations of Christian theologians. As evident in the distinct ways the Synoptic Gospels, John's Gospel, and the Epistles of Paul approach the story of Jesus Christ, such differences are present in the work of the original theologians who authored Scripture itself. On the one hand, from the very beginning, the Christian faith was one, a single vision of flourishing life, because there was one Jesus Christ, the one Word of God made flesh in a single human being (John 1:14). On the other hand, that single vision was from the start articulated and lived out in partly differing ways. Just as Jesus Christ himself lived at a given time and in a given place with a specific culture and tradition, so time, place, culture, and tradition mark the life of the church; existing in the power of the Spirit of Christ, the church lives in many diverse times and places and speaks many languages (Acts 2:1–12). The diversity of theological visions of flourishing life—even the existence of its rival versions—is in principle not a limitation but a strength, a consequence of Christian faith having taken root in the ever-changing lives of humans, all of them creatures of specific times and places. We will return to the salutary diversity of flourishing lives under the image of "improvisation" (see chap. 4).

If it is plausible to read both the original Christian theologians and their great followers through the centuries as theologians of flourishing life, then what we are proposing here is not really new but the old way of doing theology, done now in a new key because of new circumstances—above all, the dominance of instrumental reason, social pluralism, and radical privatization of the good life, all of which contribute to the waning of cultural interest in the "truth of our existence" and therefore to the sidelining of truth-seeking conversation about this most important question of

---

been inclined to see each of these lives as an example of varieties of the flourishing life rooted in particular gifts and callings that a particular individual may have.

our lives (see chap. 1). Below the surface, though, interest in the question remains strong as many of us sense that our very selves and the future of our world are at stake.

The Purpose of Theology and Its Subject Matter

To say that theology should serve flourishing life is to make a statement about the *purpose* of theology. We engage in theological endeavor because we desire to discern, articulate, and commend a vision of flourishing life in light of Jesus Christ in a given time and place. But what about the *subject matter* of theology—that on which theology focuses so as to achieve its purpose?

The subject matter of theology will depend on the basic character of flourishing life. Questions of theological method, including the purpose and subject matter of theology, are always closely tied to questions of theological substance. As we will argue shortly, the flourishing life of human beings and of the entire creation is their existence as the "home of God"—the kind of existence that depends on creation coming to itself by becoming a dwelling place of God. This conviction is at the heart of our specific proposal about how to understand flourishing life as the purpose of theology. As we have indicated earlier, other visions are possible and legitimate.

To embrace *this account of flourishing* and to claim that the purpose of theology is flourishing life is to imply that two significant ways Christian theologians have construed the subject matter of their discipline are inadequate. First, though we are theologians for God's sake,[2] Christian theology shouldn't be mainly about God because the mission of God isn't mainly about God—neither about God apart from the world (*theologia* in the patristic sense) nor about God in God's relation to the world (*oikonomia* in the patristic sense). To make this claim is decidedly *not* to say either that God is not the cornerstone theme of theology or even that theology has no business reflecting on God's own being apart from God's relation to the world. Second, Christian theology shouldn't

2. Jürgen Moltmann, *Theology and the Future of the Modern World* (Pittsburgh: ATS, 1995), 1.

be primarily about the redeeming relation of God to the world, whether we mean by redemption forgiveness of sins or liberation from suffering and oppression, or both together. This is decidedly *not* to say that redemption isn't an indispensable and central theological theme.

Why are these two ways of understanding theology's subject matter inadequate—again, inadequate assuming the account of flourishing we advocate here (which, as we have noted, is not the only possible or legitimate account)? Given that the first of all the commandments is to love the one true God above all things (Mark 12:28–30), why not make theology about God, as the word itself—"the study of God"—suggests and as many great theologians throughout Christian history insist? Alternatively, given that one of the earliest summaries of the Christian faith tersely states "that Christ died for our sins . . . and was raised on the third day in accordance with the scriptures" (1 Cor. 15:3–4), why not center theology on the relation between God who saves humans from their sins and the humans who are saved, as the great Reformer Martin Luther did?

We will develop our proposal by answering the last two questions, one after the other. In the process, we hope to also alleviate a worry that our proposal is likely to generate among some theologians who, like us, are committed to the divinity of God: a suspicion that making flourishing life the purpose of theology pushes God to the margins or, perhaps worse, that it makes God a tool we construct and use to serve our ends—namely, the world's flourishing. We share the concern. To marginalize or to instrumentalize God would be to undo the divinity of God and to secularize the world.[3] But we deny that the concern applies to our proposal. Even theologians who believe, as we do, that however much *speech* about God can be marginalized and instrumentalized, *God* cannot be, even such theologians should make flourishing life the purpose

---

3. For a powerful critique of the instrumentalization of God, see the insistence of Karl Barth in his early work that God is the Lord who rules rather than a servant who does what the master needs doing. Karl Barth, *Church Dogmatics*, I/I, trans. G. W. Bromiley (Edinburgh: T&T Clark, 1975).

of their theological endeavors for the simple reason that flourishing life is God's purpose in creating the world.

Other theologians will celebrate theology that makes the life of the world its main concern. But some of them may bristle at the sketch we offer here of a positive vision of a flourishing life with a claim to be true for all human beings. Echoing a widespread cultural sensibility, they reject any determinate positive personal and social vision as exclusionary. We will take up this second worry in chapter 4.

God

Likely the greatest of all postbiblical Christian theologians, Thomas Aquinas, stated unequivocally at the beginning of his *Summa Theologiae* that the beatitude of human beings—that which gives them unadulterated happiness and realizes their human fullness—"cannot possibly be in any created good" but must be "found in God alone."[4] Many have interpreted Thomas to mean that "alone" is here the critical word: the joy of the blessed is God alone, not any created goods alongside of, or even in, God. Correspondingly, theology has ultimately one object alone: God. Everything that is created comes under theology's domain only insofar as it has God as its "beginning" and, importantly, "end."[5] Theology ought to concentrate on God because it seeks to explain why and how human beings, creatures as they are, find beatitude in God alone. This interpretation of Thomas is contested. Whether or not Thomas held this view, we invoke it here because it reflects an important strand in Christian theology.[6]

4. Thomas Aquinas, *Summa Theologiae* I-II.2.8, contra.
5. Aquinas, *Summa Theologiae* I.1.7.
6. One of the most consistent proponents of this strand of theology was Gregory of Nyssa. The goal of the human journey—the content of flourishing for the kind of beings humans are created to be—is infinite growth in God. The hope of the blessed has nothing to do with the world but consists in the being of God. God's end for human beings is "one, and one only; it is this: when the complete whole of

The claim that the ultimate human end is God alone stands in unresolvable tension with Thomas's conviction that in the world to come humans will enjoy not only the vision of God, but also communion with one another, and they will do so as bodily beings, which helps explain why this reading of Thomas is contested.[7] It also stands in tension with Jesus's life and teachings. As recorded in the Synoptic Gospels, the very center of Jesus's mission, "God's good news,"[8] as Mark 1:14 puts it, was not God alone but the coming of the kingdom of God, the signs of which were, for those who had eyes to see, evident as events in the world: in Jesus's teaching not just about love for God but about, for instance, wealth, sex, food, and power; in the miracles of healing and feeding he performed; and in the community he gathered and the modest but joyous feast they celebrated.[9]

---

our race shall have been perfected from the first man to the last . . . to offer to every one of us participation in the blessings which are in Him, which, the Scripture tells us, 'eye hath not seen, nor ear heard,' nor thought ever reached. But this is nothing else, as I at least understand it, but to be in God Himself; for the Good which is above hearing and eye and heart must be that Good which transcends the universe." Gregory of Nyssa, *De anima et resurrectione*, in *Nicene and Post-Nicene Fathers*, Series 2, vol. 5, *Gregory of Nyssa: Dogmatic Treatises*, trans. William Moore and Henry Austin Wilson (1893; repr., New York: Cosimo, 2007), 465.

7. Germain Grisez has argued that Thomas is inconsistent on the matter and that the inconsistency needs to be resolved by giving up the idea that human ultimate fulfillment is in God alone. To be genuinely fulfilled, human beings need to be fulfilled "with respect to all the goods proper to their nature" and therefore not through God alone (Germain Grisez, "The True Ultimate End of Human Beings: The Kingdom, Not God Alone," *Theological Studies* 69 [2008]: 38–61). It is possible and likely correct to read Thomas as in fact claiming what Grisez argues that he should be claiming (as Adam Eitel related in personal communication with the authors).

8. Authors' translation.

9. Let's not trip over the male and inherently hierarchical word "king" as used for God. For neither is God male nor is God's "power," among other powers in the world, a particularly impressive power that is by far greater than any other and all others combined. God is beyond the distinction of male and female, and God's power, like Christ's rule, is "not from this world" (John 18:36), which is to say that it is categorically different from any created power. If we take Jesus's life and teaching as revelatory of the nature of God's "kingship," it is clear that the heart of this power is so different from what we often take to be "power" but instead appears to our eyes as *service* (Mark 10:45).

Scholars have often debated whether the phrase "kingdom of God," one of the dominant images of flourishing life in the Bible, refers to God's rule or realm. But it would be misleading, if not false, to consider these as mutually exclusive alternatives. When the dust settles after intricate debates about the absolute and relative attributes of God or about the "monarchy" of the Father, in our view, the claim still holds: without some kind of a realm, God would rule over nothing, which is to say that God wouldn't rule at all. Inversely, and less controversially: without the rule, the realm would not be God's and God would not be God in it. God was not the "king" before the creation of heaven and earth; God became the "king"—the Master of the Universe, as *Adon Olam*, the ancient Jewish hymn, puts it—when God created what is other than God (even if it is true that throughout history God ruled and continues to rule over unwilling and often self-destructively seditious subjects). The creation of the world is the beginning of God's rule over the realm consisting in everything that is not God; the consummation of the world is the fullness of God's rule.

The most basic and the most consequential conviction about the kingdom of God is the obvious one: it is neither kingdom alone (a world apart from God) nor God alone (God without the world), but the two together. The kingdom of God that Jesus proclaimed and enacted is a particular kind of *dynamic relation* between God and the world: it is "the world-with-God" and "God-with-the world." The kingdom of God that Jesus as Emmanuel himself *was*—Origen's *autobasileia*[10]—is God-with-us and we-with-God. Human beings and the world come to fulfillment when they become in actuality what they have always been in intention: when God rules the world in such a way that God and the world are "at home" with each other—

10. Origen, *Commentary on Matthew*, in *Ante-Nicene Fathers*, vol. 9, ed. Allan Menzies, trans. John Patrick (Buffalo, NY: Christian Literature Publishing Co., 1896), book 14, chap. 7. See Hans Urs von Balthasar, ed., *Origen: Spirit and Fire; A Thematic Anthology of His Writings*, trans. Robert J. Daly, SJ (Washington, DC: Catholic University of America Press, 1984), §1017, p. 362; Joseph Ratzinger, *Jesus of Nazareth: From the Baptism in the Jordan to the Transformation*, trans. Adrian J. Walker (New York: Doubleday, 2007), 49.

more precisely, when God comes to dwell in the world and when the world has become and experiences itself as being God's home.

The image of the home of God as an abiding relation between God and the world fits well with two great images bookending the Bible. Both are images of the creation's wholeness and flourishing. At the beginning of the Bible, there is a story of a *verdant garden* (Gen. 2:4–3:22). The garden was the world in a particular state—humans living and working in peace with all other thriving creatures, flora and fauna. But the garden, with everything in it including humans and their work of "tilling and keeping" (2:15), was not a self-standing reality. It was dependent both on God as the creator and sustainer and, less fundamentally but critically, on human recognition of God as the giver of life, a point that both God's prohibition from eating the fruit of the one tree and God's daily visits to the garden underscored.[11]

Reading Genesis and Exodus together makes manifest that God's aim both with creation of the world and with liberation of the children of Israel from Egyptian slavery was to create a space of God's presence with the people. The story that begins with creation comes to its goal with God's coming to dwell in the tabernacle: "Then the cloud covered the tent of meeting, and the glory of the Lord filled the tabernacle" (Exod. 40:34). The tabernacle, with God's presence in it, completes the creation. Or rather, it is a central moment in the history of making the entire world "into a space in which God's presence can be concretely experienced," as Bernd Janowski has put it.[12]

The other image, at the end of the Bible, is of a *thriving (and verdant!) city* (Rev. 21:1–22:7). In the vision of John the Seer, it appears exceedingly rich in cultural and material goods, placed in

---

11. For such reading of the prohibition, see Miroslav Volf, *Free of Charge* (Grand Rapids: Zondervan, 2005), 93–96.

12. Bernd Janowski, "Die Einwohnung Gottes in Israel," in *Das Geheimnis der Gegenwart Gottes: Zur Schechina-Vorstellung in Judentum und Christentum*, ed. Bernd Janowski and Enno E. Popkes (Tübingen: Mohr Siebeck, 2014), 23. On the relation between creation, the exodus, and the institutionalization of God's presence, see Jan Assmann, *Exodus: Die Revolution der Alten Welt* (Munich: Beck, 2015), 48–50, 343–60.

a healthy ecosystem and utterly secure. But the city is not a self-standing reality, a world without God or even apart from God. On the one hand, the entire city is an immense "holy of holies," the most sacred site of God's most intense presence in the temple. On the other hand, God and the Lamb are the temple in which the holy of holies is situated[13]—the omnipresent God in the ambiance of the world become God's home. This last phrase echoes the central claim of John the Evangelist that Jesus Christ, the Word incarnate, is God at home in human flesh, having come into the world to remake the world into God's home (John 1:14).[14]

As the identity, proclamation, and practice of Jesus along with the images of the primal garden and the eschatological city suggest, God's goal for the world and for humanity is not God. God's goal for the world is the *world*—though not a secular world apart from God but the world with God as a residing "owner" rather than absentee "landlord," the world having come truly into its own and flourishing by having become God's home.

The first and most important Christian theologian, the apostle Paul, stated at the summit of his most important work that all things are from God and through God and for God (Rom. 11:36). Paraphrasing this all-encompassing claim, we can say: all things were created by God; all things continue to exist through God; and all things are destined to become God's home. At the end of history, when Jesus hands over the kingdom to God the Father, God will be "all in all," wrote the same theologian (1 Cor. 15:28). How? Not by the world and each human drowning in the vast Ocean that is God,[15] nor by God becoming the sole object of human attention and joy, but by the entire creation flourish-

13. See Miroslav Volf, *After Our Likeness: The Church as the Image of the Trinity* (Grand Rapids: Eerdmans, 1998), 128.

14. The verbal resonance in Greek can be missed in English translation. Revelation 21:3: "See, the home [*skēnē*] of God is among mortals. He will dwell [*skēnōsei*] with them." John 1:14: "And the Word became flesh and lived [*eskēnōsen*] among us."

15. So recently Katherine Sonderegger, "God and the Good Life," paper presented at the Yale Center for Faith and Culture conference on the Future of Theology, New Haven, CT, June 9–10, 2016, 10.

ing in all its richness as it finds itself fully at home with itself by God dwelling in it.

For the Christian faith and therefore also for Christian theology, the question about the flourishing life is always and decisively a question about God—more specifically, about the creator, redeemer, and consummator whose self-revelation is Jesus Christ. Without God, the giver of life, everything shrivels and dies (cf. Gen. 2:7; Ezek. 37:1–14; John 20:22). The inverse is true as well: for the Christian faith and therefore also for Christian theology, the question about God, who in Christ has taken on human life and destiny in order to bring creation to its consummation as God's home, is always and inescapably the question about truly flourishing life. To imagine flourishing life without God is to embrace false immanence, an impossible God-less creation; to affirm God without relating God to flourishing life is to embrace false transcendence, an impossible God of love who is nonetheless indifferent to the work of God's own hands.

If this account of flourishing life is compelling, then the subject of theology is not God, whether in Godself or as the origin and goal of creatures, but God as the creator and consummator coming to indwell the world *and* the world as God's creation and God's home. The purpose of theology is then to help human beings identify God's home as their home and to help us journey toward it. The key aspect of the journey is redemption from oppression and sin.

But should not theology then be primarily about redemption?

Redemption

In his lectures on Psalm 51, Martin Luther stated that "the proper subject of theology is man guilty of sin and condemned, and God the Justifier and Savior of man the sinner."[16] A theologian, then, ought to explore all topics in relation to the place of the human

16. Martin Luther, "Psalm 51," in *Luther's Works* (St. Louis: Concordia, 1955), 12:311.

being, as sinner and justified, before God. This is because for Luther the Christian faith is about the justification of the ungodly through Christ's righteousness, the presupposition of which is awareness of their own ungodliness. "All Scripture points to this, that God commends His kindness to us and in His Son restores to righteousness and life the nature that has fallen into sin and condemnation."[17] The Christian faith and therefore Christian theology are primarily about redemption, or so many have interpreted Luther.

It would be a mistake, however, to center the Christian faith and Christian theology on redemption or, even more narrowly, on justification. True, Jesus came calling people to repent and believe the good news. But the good news did not merely concern what Luther, following the apostle Paul, called the "inner person" captive to sin, though this was certainly and essentially part of it.[18] It very much concerned the "outer person" as well and the circumstances of human life: ordinary poverty, hunger, sickness, oppression, captivity, and so on (see Matt. 5:3–12; Luke 4:18–19; 6:20–26), dimensions of Christ's work that Luther, to be consistent, transmuted into symbols for God's transformation of the "inner person."[19] More importantly, Jesus didn't proclaim that life will be merely repaired as the kingdom of God is being established, though, of course, much repair was needed. Nor did he simply enact a new way of repairing life, notably through transformation of the self and through sacrificial love, at times even to the point of death, though certainly new ways of repairing, those mentioned and others, were needed. The central and most revolutionary part of his message was an alternative vision of flourishing life—of the kingdom of God itself—rooted in God's character as universal, unconditional, and

17. Luther, "Psalm 51," in *Luther's Works*, 12:311.

18. Since Krister Stendahl's famous essay ("The Apostle Paul and the Introspective Conscience of the West," *Harvard Theological Review* 56, no. 3 [July 1963]: 199–215), it has been debated whether in so doing Luther is in fact following Paul or whether he is following what Stendahl claims was an Augustinian innovation in the interpretation of Paul.

19. For the discussion of the "materiality of salvation" in relation to Luther, see Miroslav Volf, "Materiality of Salvation," *Journal of Ecumenical Studies* 26 (1989): 447–67.

omnipotent love. This new vision informed what constitutes that from which humans need redemption; for instance, rather than considering "impurity" as sin, Jesus considered absence of love toward those who were deemed impure as sin (Luke 8:42–48; 11:37–44). The new vision also shaped how the work of "repair" was to take place; for instance, he taught that it cannot occur through the use of violence against wrongdoers but must occur through the bearing of their sin and the transformation of their entire selves (Matt. 5:21–26, 38–48; Mark 10:35–45; John 1:29; 3:1–10).

Redemption, or the repair of the human condition, is the Christian faith's subsidiary theme, contingent on the actuality of brokenness and sin in history. Its two primary themes are creation (expressed paradigmatically in the image of the garden of Eden) and consummation (expressed paradigmatically in the image of the new Jerusalem).

The claim that redemption is a subsidiary theme will surprise those familiar mainly with accounts of the Christian faith construed along the axis of sin and redemption. But sin and redemption cannot stand independently of creation and consummation. For sin and redemption presuppose some fundamental good from which humanity has fallen and toward which humanity needs to be (re)oriented or into which humanity needs to be set. "Redemption"

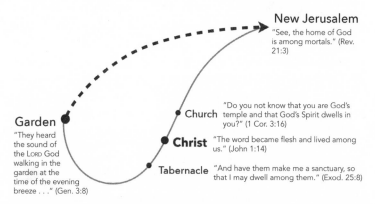

Figure 3.1 Primary and subsidiary biblical narrative arcs with significant biblical images of the "home of God."

as a removal of a lack (i.e., of sin or of evil) is always a means, never the final end. Redemption helps us get where we are meant to be, but the vision of life established through creation and promised in consummation sets the destination; redemption is a condition of consummation and an effect of the consummation's inauguration.

The purpose of the Christian faith and therefore also of theology is not merely to liberate people from captivity to the negative so as to place them in a neutral space from which they can then go wherever they wish; it is to free them from the negative so as to place them in the *positive*, or, more precisely, it is to free them from the negative *by* placing them in the positive. Nor is its goal to free people from the negative so as to return them to an original pristine state from which they had fallen. There is forward movement toward the "new thing" in God's story with the world: the end fits the beginning but does not replicate it; a cultivated garden becomes an ecologically sound, culturally rich, and utterly secure city. In the Synoptic Gospels, as we have seen, God's good news is that the "time is fulfilled" and that the "kingdom of God has come near"; the coming of this new thing necessitates and gives character to repentance (Mark 1:14–15). In Paul, the faithfulness of Christ and the reality of the new creation in which humans participate by faith are the good; "salvation" is not mere removal of the negative, however understood (condemnation, futility, loss of divine glory, etc.), but placement into the realm of the positive (union with Christ, new creation). In John's Gospel, finally, the Word comes to dwell among humans not merely so that Jesus Christ as the Lamb of God can take "away the sin of the world" (John 1:29) but, ultimately, so that the Word can be, in an unimpeded way, the life and the light of the world made to be God's home (1:1–17).[20]

20. When it comes to moral theology, rather than a Christian account of redemption, the situation is similar: though the law is formulated primarily in negative terms, as a series of denials at the heart of which is the command to have "no other gods" (Exod. 20:3), from Jesus's and Paul's summaries of the law, it is clear that the law's intention is to direct lives toward a positive good—the law calls for a positive relation (love) toward an object understood as ultimate or proximate good (e.g., God, neighbor).

Martin Luther is as plain as can be that the Christian faith (and therefore theology) should be centered on redemption, on removal of guilt, and on justification. And yet, arguably, even for him, the removal of the negative (i.e., freedom from guilt on account of inability to love God and neighbor perfectly) is not the goal; the freedom to love God and neighbor through Christ's indwelling is, as his *The Freedom of a Christian* indicates.[21] In fact, the removal of the negative is not even an independent means of achieving the goal but a *consequence* of the union with Christ, a state for which human beings were created in the first place.[22] Luther was, arguably, a theologian of love, and he was a theologian of redemption because he was a theologian of love.[23]

The problem with Luther's account of the Christian faith and of theology is that he distinguishes too sharply between the "inner person" and the "outer person" and, correspondingly, also too sharply between the "law" and the "gospel." He therefore could not quite see the transformation of the world into God's home as the goal of God's ways with creation. Christian faith and Christian theology aren't simply about freedom from guilt and love for God and neighbors; they are about more encompassing flourishing life, of which freedom from guilt and love for God and neighbors are essential parts.

Jesus Christ, God's Home

Jesus Christ—in his person, his life, and his mission—is both the embodiment of God's home among mortals and the promise of its full and universal realization. That, we think, is implied in the great line from the beginning of John's Gospel summing up the

21. See Martin Luther, "The Freedom of a Christian," in *Luther's Works* (Philadelphia: Fortress, 1957), 31:327–78.

22. See especially Luther's comments in *Lectures on Galatians* in *Luther's Works* (St. Louis: Concordia, 1963), 26:167–68.

23. For an argument that Luther was a theologian of love, see Ronald R. Rittgers, "Martin Luther and the Reformation of Love: The Heart of the Protestant Revolution," Mark A. Noll inaugural lecture, 2017 (unpublished manuscript).

entire mission of Jesus Christ: "The Word became flesh and dwelt among us" (John 1:14 RSV). As God-with-us, to use the name given to the as-of-yet unborn Jesus as his destiny (Matt. 1:23; cf. Isa. 7:14), Jesus Christ *was* God at home in mortal flesh. His mission, undertaken in the power of the same Spirit through whose overshadowing of Mary his very identity was established (Luke 1:35; 4:1, 14), was to make the whole world God's home and thus creatures' true home, the site of their true flourishing. The life of Christians and Christian communities, constituted by the Spirit, is the continuation of Christ's anointing by the Spirit to participate in Christ's life and mission.[24] The purpose of Christian theology is the flourishing of all life because Christian theology stands in service of the continuation of Christ's mission to embody and spread the good news of God's coming to make the world into God's home.

Primary and Secondary Flourishing

But what exactly can "flourishing life" mean if Christ is its prime exemplar, its archetype? In its primary sense, the flourishing life is identical with what Jesus Christ *announced* to have come near and toward which his entire mission was aiming: the kingdom of God in its fullness, the realized hope of Israel's prophets (see, e.g., Isa. 40:9–11). In the terminology of the apostle Paul, it is the new creation in Christ, a world of "justice, peace, and joy in the Holy Spirit" (Rom. 14:17), as we will explicate in detail in chapter 6. In the imagery of John the Seer, it is the new Jerusalem, the city rich in cultural and natural goods, but existing as the temple of God; it is the world as God's home (Rev. 21:3). Then and there, in the new world that comes from God, all God's creatures will flourish in God's presence; the flourishing of each will aid the flourishing of all, and the flourishing of all will in fact be an aspect of the flourishing of each. This is the flourishing life in its ultimate form, in the world become God's home.

24. See Miroslav Volf and Maurice Lee, "The Spirit and the Church," in "Miroslav Volf," special issue, *The Conrad Grebel Review* 18, no. 3 (2000): 20–45. See also Miroslav Volf and Ryan McAnnally-Linz, *Public Faith in Action* (Grand Rapids: Brazos, 2016).

In its secondary sense, flourishing life is what Christ *enacted in his own life in the course of his mission to announce the nearness of God's rule.* For Christ's followers as well, flourishing life in this secondary sense is his kind of life transposed, in the power of the Spirit, from first-century Palestine into multiple settings in diverse times and places with their technological and cultural peculiarities. This is the flourishing life in its penultimate form, on the way to the world becoming God's home and engaged in the struggle of helping to make the world into God's home. What Jesus Christ announced was enacted in his life and in the effects of his mission, and these enactments were a light, a bright but flickering light, that shone in darkness; they were events in a world that very much wasn't the kingdom of God but a space occupied by Rome, a most visible and palpable instantiation of the more fine-grained, pervasive, and enduring presence of the powers of evil.

As "God-with-us," Christ served his fellow human beings by proclaiming God's coming in word and deed: he alleviated the plight of the poor, sick, oppressed, and those ridden by guilt and covered in shame for having failed to love God and neighbor; and he liberated those caught in the snares of power, wealth, and self-righteousness. All this he did in the power of the Spirit and

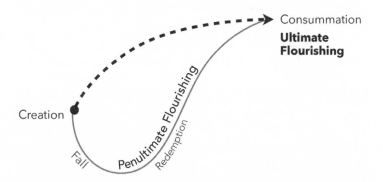

Figure 3.2 Primary and subsidiary biblical narrative arcs. The top arc depicts the creation-consummation main plot, which was intended from the foundation of the world; the bottom depicts the sin-redemption subplot that deals with the contingency of sin. The top, main arc attracts the bottom arc and norms it.

with utter dedication to God, nourished by practices of prayer and fasting. Some of his fellow compatriots were drawn into his mission; they became friends with whom he shared meals and celebrated feasts in the company of the outcasts. In all this he, his disciples, and those he attracted had foretastes of the coming world, of truly flourishing life. On occasion, like on the Mount of Transfiguration, the new world flashed in its glory in the midst of the false life of the present world (Luke 9:28–36).

But aren't we forgetting his inglorious death? After fewer than three years of ministry, the authorities and, ultimately, the majority of people violently rejected Jesus Christ. All along, many derided and persecuted him because he disregarded some common moral sensibilities (Luke 7:34) and broke the law where it did not serve humans (6:1–5). To those who were repelled, Jesus's way of life looked like that of a blasphemer of God, in part because he tied his own person too closely with God's (22:66–71). He was seen as a threat to national survival and a rebel against Roman imperial rule (John 19:12–15). He was apprehended, tortured, and condemned to a brutal and untimely death. His disciples abandoned him, and, according to Matthew's Gospel, his own last words as he was dying expressed an even deeper sense of abandonment: "My God, my God, why have you forsaken me?" (Matt. 27:46).

Was this a flourishing life? Was this God having made God's home in human flesh? Seen from one angle, it was a well-meaning but misguided burst of energy, a failed life of self-inflicted languishing and premature death. No other great paradigmatic figure in the history of humanity—not the Buddha, not Confucius, not Socrates, not Muhammad—lived such a short and seemingly tragic life. From the perspective of the life of the kingdom Jesus announced, too, his life seemed a failure. That's how his original followers saw it: the failure of his life seemed to falsify the claim to the goodness of his own cause (Luke 24:21). But did it? Was it a failure, a futile life and a pointless death? If it wasn't, as Christians believe, might not the way he lived and died, the entirety of his life, have been a mode of flourishing, too—especially in light of his resurrection and exaltation?

True Life within the False

In *Minima Moralia*, the German philosopher Theodor Adorno famously asked whether there can be true life in the false one.[25] This is a critical question for all who embrace the idea of the "true life"—truly flourishing life—as Christians do. Are there modes of authentic flourishing in a world that, on account of its basic structures and fundamental orientation, isn't flourishing itself? Adorno insisted that there is no true life in the false, damaged life. Followers of Christ are committed to disagreeing with Adorno. Flourishing life in the primary and ultimate sense is the true life; flourishing life in the secondary and penultimate sense is *the mode of the true life under the conditions of the false life*. First, in Christ's life some of the truly flourishing life (e.g., feasting and friendship, joy and purity of heart, and in all of this utter dedication to God) shines through despite struggle and suffering; but even the light of a firefly is a light, though only a brief and weak flash in the enveloping darkness. Second, suffering and apparent failure were, in Christ's life, intimately related to the true flourishing life. They were *means* to flourishing life, fully in service of the kingdom of God. Perhaps more importantly, as means to flourishing life they were fractured reflections, echoes of the flourishing life itself, garbled by the pervasive sin and constitutional fragility of the world.

What unites in Christ's life both the brief and bitterly sweet delights of love, peace, and joy (flashes of the flourishing life in the primary sense) and the more abiding struggle and suffering (hard labor of helping the world become the site of true flourishing) is this: they are the fruit of the same unconditional love of God that flows as the fount of all reality. Flourishing in the primary sense is an enactment of divine love in a world in which the aims of love have been realized because the world has become God's home; in response to God's love, all in that world practice undiluted love toward God and all creatures, all live in peace

---

25. Theodor Adorno, *Minima Moralia: Reflections on a Damaged Life*, trans. E. F. N. Jephcott (New York: Verso, 2005), §18, p. 39.

with God and creation, and all inhabit a space of joy, God's and humans'. Flourishing in the secondary sense is also an enactment of unconditional love—not just in the flashes of true life in the midst of the false one but most decidedly also in the pain and suffering associated with the struggle for the world to become God's home.

As it is in Christ's life, so it is, analogously, in God's life: the love of the Triune God after the world has finally and definitely become God's home is love that dances; the love of the Triune God on the journey of redemption through history is love that often has to suffer.[26] As it is in God's life and Christ's life, so it is, analogously, in the lives of those called and empowered by the Spirit to be "Christs" to the world and to participate in Christ's mission[27]—except that they, too, are part of the world that has not yet fully become God's home. A tension marks the life they live in this world, a struggle, internal and private as well as social, even structural, and public, for the true life in the midst of the false one.

Why should Christian theology be about flourishing life and serve flourishing life? Because Christ came to call people to flourishing life. Guided by God's kind of love and empowered by God's Spirit, all of us are called to flourish fully in the world-become-God's-home and partially on the journey there—rejoicing even while having to mourn, accepting lack willingly so that the needs of others can be satisfied, leading lives of courage and integrity as we struggle against the evils of this age, trusting and loving God, participating in God's mission in the world, and in all this growing into our own human fullness.

---

26. On the two forms of God's love toward the world, see Miroslav Volf, "'The Trinity Is Our Social Program': The Doctrine of the Trinity and the Shape of Social Engagement," *Modern Theology* 14, no. 3 (July 1998): 403–23. See also Linn Tonstad, "Sexual Difference and Trinitarian Death: Cross, Kenosis, and Hierarchy in the Theo-Drama," *Modern Theology* 26, no. 4 (October 2010): 603–31. This represents an alternative to von Balthasar, for whom suffering is part of the life of the immanent Trinity.

27. On being "Christ" to one's neighbor, see Martin Luther, "Heidelberg Disputation," in *Luther's Works* (Philadelphia: Fortress, 1957), 31:55–56.

———— **A Theology of the Flourishing Life** ————

In attending to its subject matter and pursuing its purpose to discern, articulate, and commend a vision of flourishing life, a compelling theology will need to satisfy at least three requirements. First, it will need to show that the vision fits well with a plausible, overarching theological interpretation of reality. Such an interpretation will have less the force of an explanation (e.g., a causal explanation of how the world came to be and how it functions) and more the character of a truthful seeing of the world *as* something (e.g., as God's creation that is destined for fulfillment through the "coming of God"[28]).

Second, it will need to show that the vision can be made plausible in light of the vast nontheological knowledge we have about the world. The main sources of rapidly expanding knowledge today are the sciences. In addition to theology's long-standing nontheological interlocutors, philosophy and the humanities, theology will have to enter into a truth-seeking conversation with the sciences; it will have to be a "science-engaged" theology.

Finally, theology ought to be able to show, in broad contours, how the vision of flourishing life it is commending ought to be lived in different stages and under different conditions of life. What does flourishing life look like for a child, for an adolescent, or for a person at the end of their life? What does it look like for the rich or for the poor—in what ways does it require each to engage in the struggle for greater justice and for gratitude? What does flourishing life look like in the cities or in the country? What does it look like in late modern capitalism, with people living and working in institutions and cultures marked, for instance, by "dynamic stabilization"?[29]

Articulating, assessing, and commending a vision of flourishing life demands the best of theology in its descriptive, normative,

28. For the theological weight of the phrase, see Jürgen Moltmann, *The Coming of God*, trans. Margaret Kohl (Minneapolis: Fortress, 2004).

29. For "dynamic stabilization" and absence of "resonance," see Hartmut Rosa, *Social Acceleration: A New Theory of Modernity*, trans. Jonathan Trejo-Mathys (New York: Columbia University Press, 2013); Hartmut Rosa, *Resonanz: Eine Soziologie der Weltbeziehung* (Berlin: Suhrkamp, 2016).

and instrumental modes, all the voices of its various subdisciplines working together in concert. What is needed is a biblically rooted,[30] patristically guided,[31] ecclesially located, and publicly engaged theology, done in critical conversation with the sciences and the various disciplines of the humanities, at the center of which is the question of the flourishing life.

Theology as . . .	Descriptive	Instrumental	Normative	
Science	+	–	–	Bare descriptive knowledge, whether historical, philosophical, sociological, etc. E.g., theology as religious studies.
Technology	–	+	–	Means to accomplish pregiven ends, out of touch with the nature of God, the traditions of the people of God, and the nature of the world. E.g., prosperity-gospel teaching.
Advocacy	–	–	+	Something like Hume's brute moral reactions. E.g., griping against what is condemned or fantasizing aloud about what is commended.

30. By using the term "biblically rooted"—rather than, say, "biblical"—we want to suggest that Christian accounts of the flourishing life, in the end, have to derive from Scripture but that they are not simply sitting on the surface of biblical texts waiting to be harvested. As an example of a biblically rooted account of flourishing life, we offer in chap. 6 the one we believe is to be found in Paul's letters. The apostle Paul will also be our main biblical source in chap. 5 (on the lives of theologians).

31. In describing our proposal as "patristically guided," we do not suggest leaping over fifteen centuries of theology, as if medieval, Reformation, and modern theologians had little to offer. But though theology in these centuries was often highly sophisticated and profound —think of Aquinas and Bonaventure or Luther and Schleiermacher—it is not direction setting in nearly the same way as patristic theology is.

Strategy	+	+	−	Evidence-based action plans with unthematized or insufficient normative underpinnings. E.g., church-growth strategy.
Activism	−	+	+	Brute moral reactions paired with elaborate implementation plans, all disconnected from truthful understanding of God and/or the world. E.g., ideological activism of various sorts.
Speculation	+	−	+	Normative knowledge divorced, even in principle, from practical application. E.g., so-called ivory-tower theology.
Theology	+	+	+	*Robust descriptive work oriented toward an actionable, livable normative vision of human flourishing.*

Table 3.1 Misconstruals of theology when its descriptive, instrumental, and normative aspects are not held in productive tension. Theology is not merely descriptive (as a science), instrumental (as a technology), or normative (as mere advocacy); it has all three aspects and is only well balanced when all three play together in concert.

We have not yet mentioned one important interlocutor for theology: other religious traditions. The character of the flourishing life is a contested question—one about which various religions and humanistic interpretations of reality contend. As we live in a pluralistic world, Christian theology is just one among the contending voices in a public debate about flourishing life. How should theologians engage in such public debate while honoring both the universal character of our own visions of flourishing and the advocates of alternative visions with whom we deeply disagree? This is the question to which we turn next.

4

The Challenge of Universality

The entire world and every person as the home of God! In a nutshell, this is the vision of flourishing life we argue Christian theology should serve. Though the image of home is deeply biblical and compelling, over the centuries theologians have also used other images to organize their articulations of the flourishing life: the "new creation" (building on the writings of Paul),[1] the "heavenly city" (building on the book of Revelation),[2] the "kingdom of God" (building on the proclamation of Jesus).[3] In chapter 6 we ourselves will explicate one variant of the New Testament vision of flourishing life using the image of the kingdom.

1. See, e.g., John Wesley, "The New Creation," in *John Wesley's Sermons: An Anthology*, ed. Albert C. Outler and Richard P. Heizenrater (Nashville: Abingdon, 1991), 493–500.
2. See, e.g., Augustine, *The City of God*, trans. Henry Bettenson (New York: Penguin, 2003).
3. See, e.g., Gustavo Gutiérrez, *Theology of Liberation*, trans. Sister Caridad Inda and John Eagleson (Maryknoll, NY: Orbis, 1988).

─────── **One God, One World, One Home** ───────

All accounts of flourishing life associated with these images—in fact, nearly all Christian accounts of flourishing life—share one important feature that has become unpalatable for many today: they claim universal validity. A Christian vision of flourishing life addresses every person and the entire world; notwithstanding humanity's and the world's lush diversity—or, better yet, *in* that diversity—the "new creation" is one; the "heavenly city," though made up of many dwellings and neighborhoods, is one; the "kingdom of God," though having many diverse regions, is one; "God's home" is one, and therefore the vision of flourishing is one. The singleness of this vision implies more than that everyone, each in their own way, ought to live it out. All humans and all life on the planet are interdependent, an interconnected ecology of relatedness, which is what the image of home expresses, perhaps, better than any other in the Bible. For one person to truly flourish, the entire world must flourish; for the entire world to truly flourish, every person in it must flourish; and for every person and the entire world to truly flourish, each in their own way and all together must live in the presence of the life-giving God.

The universality of the Christian vision of flourishing follows from the oneness of God. The one God is the abiding source of all creatures and therefore the God of every human being and of the entire world. Correspondingly, the divine Word, who became incarnate in Jesus Christ, enlightens every person, and as the Lamb of God that same Word-become-flesh bears the sin of the whole world (John 1:9, 29). Jesus Christ is, as John's Gospel famously puts it, "the way, and the truth, and the life" (14:6). One way of life is true for all, even if each person walks it in his or her own way; the destination is one, even though there are many dwelling places in it (14:2).

From one angle, universality is all-encompassing inclusivity: everything comes from the one God, and therefore everything flourishes in God's home. But the obverse of monotheism's total inclusivity is a certain kind of exclusivity. Now, there are all-inclusive forms of monotheism ("all gods are One"), but today's major monotheisms are all exclusive ("no god but the One").[4] This is true of Islam: "No god but God" are the very first words of the most basic Islamic profession of faith. It is also true of Judaism, the tradition that gave the world the gift of allegiance to one God: "You shall have no other gods before me" is the key prohibition of the very first of the Ten Commandments (Exod. 20:3). Christianity is no different from Judaism in this regard: "No God but One," writes Paul in 1 Corinthians 8:4, repeating in his own way his Jewish ancestors' commitment to God's unicity. A negation is a necessary obverse of the affirmation of a universal vision of flourishing rooted in God's oneness. The one true God is distinguished from many false gods;[5] one true way of life (or multiple true ways of life[6]) is distinguished from false ways of life.

The Scandal of Universality

The universality of the vision of flourishing that theology seeks to articulate pushes against an important cultural sensibility prevalent in the contemporary West. Many of us have come to think that categories of "true" and "false" do not properly apply to religion; instead, we assess religion in aesthetic or utilitarian terms, placing

4. On inclusive monotheism (which establishes a connection between God and gods and comes about through evolution of ideas) and the exclusive monotheism of the Bible (which draws a distinction between God and gods and comes about through "revolution") see Jan Assmann, *Of God and Gods: Egypt, Israel, and the Rise of Monotheism* (Madison: University of Wisconsin Press, 2008), 53–75.

5. See Assmann, *Of God and Gods*, 106–11; Assmann, *The Price of Monotheism*, trans. Robert Savage (Stanford, CA: Stanford University Press, 2010). In *Exodus: Die Revolution der Alten Welt* (Munich: Beck, 2015), Assmann qualifies his thesis somewhat with regard to biblical monotheism, which he characterizes as monotheism of faithfulness rather than monotheism of truth. But as long as the claim that God is one is valid, faithfulness is faithfulness to the one true God in contrast to realities that, by definition, cannot be God, and the problem of exclusivity, if it is a problem, returns.

6. The one true God can be the source of multiple true ways of life. Jewish tradition distinguishes between Mosaic law, which applies only to the Jews, and the Noachide laws, which apply to the gentiles. For a Jewish articulation of how the one God is the source of difference, see Jonathan Sacks, *The Dignity of Difference: How to Avoid the Clash of Civilizations* (New York: Continuum, 2002).

a religion as a whole, or aspects of its teaching and practice, on the spectrum from attractive to repugnant or from useful to harmful (see chap. 1).[7] We do the same with accounts of flourishing life more broadly. Consequently, a particular account may be good or true for me but need not be good or true for you or someone else; and if it is good or true for me today, it need not be so tomorrow.

As many of us see it, the sciences, not religions or philosophies of life, stand for truth in contrast to falsehood (though even scientific truths are likely to be put in quotation marks and declared to be merely the positions of a lobby group when they impinge on our preferred way of life).[8] Some are convinced that the sciences can provide us with foundations of morality—that is, define for us our human purpose. Yet despite the immense amount of intellectual work done to shore up that conviction, the position remains implausible.[9] Scientific research, a fantastic tool, is *driven by* purposes and values, but it is *about* facts and explanations and cannot set purposes and define values. It can tell us a lot, for instance, about what humans tend to desire and why and how to achieve their goals more effectively but not much about what they ought to desire and why or what kind of life is worth desiring. There is no truth or falsehood about the ends of our lives, we tend to think. In the domain of purposes and values, we are free, ultimately, to do as we please, provided we don't harm others (an important condition but ambiguous, too, because it wrongly assumes that we agree on what constitutes "harm").

7. To assess religions on the basis of usefulness invites immediately the question, "Useful for what?" If we think of a religion as useful for the kind of life that that religion itself does not define, we operate with a conception of religions as mere "means." That is a possible way of conceiving religion, especially as many practice religion in just that way. But one forgets then that one of the constitutive features of great religions is to define the ultimate end of human lives.

8. See Bruno Latour, *An Inquiry into Modes of Existence: An Anthropology of the Moderns*, trans. Catherine Porter (Cambridge, MA: Harvard University Press, 2013), 2–5.

9. For a recent argument, see James Davidson Hunter and Paul Nedelisky, *Science and the Good: The Tragic Quest for the Foundations of Morality* (New Haven: Yale University Press, forthcoming).

A sharp contrast between truths of science and arbitrary beliefs of religion is untenable. Still, even those who grant this point often consider the idea of truth about the direction of our lives and the corresponding "tables of value" problematic. They worry that a life deemed universally "true" will likely not fit who we see ourselves to be as individuals at any given time or that it will interfere with our choosing the life we want.[10] They fear that it may push us to undervalue or despise those who do not live "in the truth." Finally, we resist commitment to truth about the good life because we fear that it will divide us into mutually intolerant groups, clashing irreconcilably as we seek to live in a common space.

In the present chapter we will address these concerns. First, we will argue that positive, substantive visions of the flourishing life are unavoidable; and as all affirmations are also denials, there is no avoiding contestation between such visions. Second, we will argue that accounts of the Christian vision of true life are available such that those who advocate them can peacefully coexist and collaborate with and even learn from people who advocate alternative visions. Finally, we will elaborate on how, properly understood, Christian visions of true life take into account the changing particularities of individual lives in specific places.

Truth Claims Too Ancient to Be Believed?

In this chapter we will leave one important task undone. We won't attempt to defend our position against critics who claim that theology, while claiming to be about truth, trades in mere beliefs—in fact, beliefs that we owe to ancient people who had a fraction of our knowledge about the world or our technological prowess. In response, we merely note the following: theology isn't *primarily* about explanatory or instrumental knowledge. If it were, it would be, as its

10. It is sometimes said that we would lose choice if we were to think of the ends of our lives and of criteria for desiring as true or false. But that isn't quite right. Opting for true life and against the false life is a choice, too. What we would lose is a particular *basis* for choosing a way of life—namely, the sufficiency of the fact that we desire it.

critics claim it is, a debunked science grounding an obsolete technology. Theology is not primarily about explanatory or instrumental knowledge because the Christian faith isn't primarily about that kind of knowledge. The Christian faith is primarily about the relation between God and the world—more specifically, about the true life in Jesus Christ, who is the revelation of God and the paradigmatic exemplar of humanity in one (though, of course, the truthfulness of what that faith says about the relation between God and the world and about the true life depends on the truthfulness of its claims about the nature of God and of Jesus Christ).

Theology as . . .	Descriptive	Instrumental	
Science	+	–	Descriptive knowledge, whether historical, philosophical, sociological, etc. E.g., theology as religious studies.
Technology	–	+	Means to accomplish pregiven ends, uninformed by the character of God, the traditions of the people of God, and the nature of the world. E.g., prosperity-gospel teaching.
Theology	+	+	*Descriptive work oriented toward a thematized normative vision of flourishing life.*

Table 4.1 Misconstruals of theology when its descriptive and instrumental aspects are not held in productive tension. Theology is not merely descriptive (as a science) or instrumental (as a technology); it has both of these aspects and is only well balanced when both work together in concert.

What exactly "truth" means when it comes to our lives—as distinct, for instance, from what "truth" means in mathematics or physics or human sciences—has been debated over the centuries, and the debates have only intensified with the rise of modern sciences.[11] However the relations among various conceptions of truth ought to be construed, if the truth of human life is found in

11. See, e.g., Stanley Hauerwas, *The State of the University: Academic Knowledges and the Knowledge of God* (Malden, MA: Blackwell, 2007).

Christ, then the direction of human striving cannot be expressions of mere personal, communal, or even civilizational preferences. People will have preferences, and we must respect their right to act on these preferences; the basic direction of one's life is ultimately a person's own responsibility.[12] But not all preferences are equal, and the purpose of Christian theology is to critically examine such preferences—indeed, to call into question our tendency to understand the decision about the direction of our entire life in terms of mere preferences—and offer compelling accounts of the Christian vision of genuinely flourishing life.[13]

The Primacy of the Positive

Before we suggest a way to articulate a Christian vision of flourishing that avoids generating social violence and suppressing individual differences, we need to close off what appears a promising alternative path to that goal but is in fact a road to nowhere. This is the view that all positive accounts of the flourishing life

---

12. On freedom of religion, see Miroslav Volf, *Flourishing: Why We Need Religion in a Globalized World* (New Haven: Yale University Press, 2015), 107–14; Miroslav Volf and Ryan McAnnally-Linz, *Public Faith in Action* (Grand Rapids: Brazos, 2016), 167–74.

13. Many modern accounts of religions downplay truth claims religions make, preferring to concentrate on the function of religious language, practices, and rituals. But these accounts tend to describe religions from an outsider's vantage point. Adherents of a particular religion overwhelmingly see the religion they embrace as making and embodying truth claims. Most of them are well aware that religion does more than that, that it has, for instance, emotional power or transformative effects, and they embrace it partly for such power and effects. Many are also cognizant of the intimate relation between practices and rituals on the one hand and internal religious states and truth claims on the other (to the effect that rituals and practices aren't mere expressions of internal states and application of truth claims). Some also sense that when we speak of the "truth of one's life tied to overarching religious interpretations of reality," we use "truth" in a distinct but no less important sense than when we speak of the truths in the context of sciences. Either way, truth claims matter; the power and effects of religion are in part—in part only!—a function of these truth claims, and rituals and practices are in part—in part only!—embodiments of these truth claims.

are complicit in generating violence and suppressing difference because they always exclude someone and do so without good reason.[14] Occasionally this view is stated as a considered intellectual position,[15] but more often it's a tacit but powerful sensibility. Those who share it maintain that we should formulate all binding conviction in negative terms.

Some would have theology follow suit. With regard to God, the basic conviction would be that all grasping is impossible "unless . . . what we grasp is the impossibility of grasping."[16] Having shunned positive statements about God, we would be left with a vague transcendence, a directionless movement of transcending. With regard to moral engagement, the primary thrust of theological work would then consist in critique designed to remove all obstacles to freedom, modalities of exclusion, and sources of suffering, the modern trinity of concerns we described in chapter 2.[17] Postcolonial sensitivities, however, drive an exception. Some critics of positive visions grant indigenous communities the right to shared "community-specific standards," knowing that without

14. We will leave aside here the most radical form of this objection: the claim that all positive determinations about the flourishing life are inimical to life, wrapping themselves too tightly around our lives and producing humans with "lotus feet." This frequent objection is an expression of the wider unease with reason that is articulated in its most extreme form by philosophers and cultural critics like Geraldine Finn but that can be traced back in the modern period to Friedrich Nietzsche. In Finn's essay collection *Why Althusser Killed His Wife: Essays on Discourse and Violence* (Atlantic Highlands, NJ: Humanities Press, 1996), she describes reason as constitutively violent and necessarily coercive because it excludes the irrational and because it constitutes a mechanism of power. Discursive reasoning has, indeed, often been placed in the service of oppressive power. At the same time, Finn's use of rational discourse in the service of liberation indicates that her categorical condemnation of discursive reasoning does not tell the whole story: the rejection of oppression is not in itself oppressive. Not all exclusion is harm, and not all assertion is violence. (Thanks to Janna Gonwa for producing this note.)

15. See, for example, John D. Caputo, *Radical Hermeneutics: Repetition, Deconstruction, and the Hermeneutic Project* (Bloomington: Indiana University Press, 1987), 240–44.

16. Mark Taylor, *About Religion: Economies of Faith in a Virtual Culture* (Chicago: University of Chicago Press, 1999), 1.

17. See also Saba Mahmood, *Politics of Piety: The Islamic Revival and the Feminist Subject* (Princeton: Princeton University Press, 2005), 13–14.

such standards communities would inevitably dissolve.[18] This exception is instructive, for if such communities are to sustain themselves, they need to engage in boundary maintenance, which in turn involves epistemic and social interventions that are otherwise seen as oppressive. To be true to itself, the critique cannot carve out space for *any* positive assertion. In the end, negation rules.

But negation's hegemony is untenable—not because we shouldn't critique sources of bondage, exclusion, and suffering, but because negation's claim to stand on its own feet is false. Despite its protestations to the contrary, negation depends on (implicit) affirmation of the positive. Behind the negative task lies a positive vision of who the self is (e.g., an autonomous individual), what relations to others should be (e.g., always mediated through individual consent and undertaken for mutual benefit), and what the good is (e.g., increase of pleasure and diminution of pain).[19] This is the irony of "pure negation": it assumes an implicit account of human nature and of the flourishing life and then contends that all positive articulations are oppressive. In the name of freedom, it denies to others what it clandestinely arrogates to itself.

Positive visions of the good life are inescapable. We can contest the nature and scope of any particular positive vision, but we cannot and should not want to eliminate all positive visions. Even liberative negations presuppose normative affirmations of individual autonomy. Similarly, we can contest particular ways and goals of crafting persons, but we cannot and should not want to eliminate the activity

18. P. J. Watson, "Transition beyond Postmodernism: Pluralistic Culture, Incommensurable Rationalities, and Future Objectivity," *Review & Expositor* 111, no. 1 (February 2014): 33–40.

19. Seyla Benhabib has persuasively argued that even the formal universalism of Kantian ethics must be founded on a respect for humanity that requires a strongly positive conception of what it means to be human. She writes: "To justify . . . respect some significantly 'thick' account of what it means to be human such that our shared humanity would matter morally and would not be limited to the likeness of 'featherless bipeds' would have to be provided, and some understanding of generalized reciprocity would have to be an aspect of any thick account of what it means to be human." Seyla Benhabib, "On Reconciliation and Respect, Justice and the Good Life: Response to Herta Nagl-Docekal and Rainer Forst," *Philosophy and Social Criticism* 23, no 5 (1997): 102.

of crafting. Even the "autonomous subjects" we might be tempted to take as "natural" are in fact the result of people having been *thus crafted* in the wake of modernity.[20] If we must operate with positive visions and craft persons, we are better off doing so explicitly, carefully, and in the company of the best of our traditions rather than implicitly and likely subject to the whims of current trends.

As to purely negative talk about God, reducing transcendence to the movement of transcending is intended to delegitimize positive visions of the good life that are deemed exclusionary and oppressive. In fact, it ends up legitimizing both the negations of the critique and the alternative positive visions of the good life that these negations necessarily presuppose. There are good reasons why theologians have, as a rule, resisted either a purely negative, apophatic approach to speech about God or a purely positive, kataphatic approach. Kataphatic and apophatic approaches are both indispensable elements in a carefully and systematically curated dialectical strategy whose purpose is both to articulate the nature of God and to acknowledge through language God's infinite transcendence of all articulations.[21] The apophatic is intelligible only as a moment within an overall approach that is always both kataphatic and apophatic, indeed, an approach that can be apophatic only because it is kataphatic.

Note that "positive" visions of flourishing life are not synonymous with "dogmatic" visions of flourishing life—in the pejorative sense of that term. Dogmatic visions are only one kind of positive visions—in fact, an inadequate and often harmful kind. As the dialectic of apophasis and kataphasis implies, there is "unknowing" in all our knowing of God, and there is "untruth" in all our legitimate truth claims about God. In the book of the prophet Isaiah, God gives the reason why unknowing is inescapable when it comes to God:

20. See Michel Foucault, "The Subject and Power," in *Power*, vol. 3 of *Essential Works of Foucault*, ed. James D. Faubion, trans. Robert Hurley et al. (New York: New Press, 2000), 326–48.
21. On the two approaches, see Denys Turner, *The Darkness of God: Negativity in Christian Mysticism* (Cambridge: Cambridge University Press, 1995).

> For my thoughts are not your thoughts,
> > nor are your ways my ways, says the LORD.
> For as the heavens are higher than the earth,
> > so are my ways higher than your ways
> > and my thoughts than your thoughts.
> > > (Isa. 55:8–9)

As it is with Christian accounts of God, so it is with Christian visions of flourishing life, partly because they concern God as their foundation and partly because they stretch out in hope toward the future. Statements of hope, too, and not just statements about God, involve unknowing. "Now hope that is seen is not hope," writes Paul (Rom. 8:24). Martin Luther took Paul's words not simply to mean that those who hope don't yet see in reality what they see with their mind's eye. Taking his cue from Paul's claim that "we do not know how to pray as we ought" (8:26), Luther thought that hope transfers a person "into the unknown, the hidden, and the dark shadow, so that he does not even know what he hopes for."[22] We can know and articulate in positive terms the Christian vision of flourishing life—and the truth of God and the truth of Jesus Christ, as well—only in a broken, unknowing kind of way, stretching ourselves toward something we see "in a mirror, dimly," and "know only in part" (1 Cor. 13:12).

Universalism without Violence

A Christian vision of flourishing life is not the only one on offer these days. Many positive visions claim to be universally valid, true for all human beings. These visions do not agree with one another, at least not on all essential points; one always denies some crucial aspects of what the other affirms. We cannot and should not try to avoid contestations among them. Nor can we, of course,

22. Martin Luther, *Lectures on Romans*, in *Luther's Works* (St. Louis: Concordia, 1972), 25:364.

simply assert our preferred vision as incontestably good. Rather, we must approach rival visions of the flourishing life, including the Christian vision, as *contending particular universalisms* and engage in a truth-seeking conversation about them.

But what exactly do we mean by "contending particular universalisms"? And, if the Christian faith is one of them, does it have internal resources to contend in a way that does not violate and oppress? In the following we take these two questions in turn, first parsing the phrase "contending particular universalism" and then sketching a way to do Christian theology in the midst of such universalisms.

Universality

Christian theologians work today in the context of multiple contending particular universalisms about the flourishing life, each with its own varieties. We call them *universalisms* not because all human beings will come to embrace them but because they make a claim to be true for all human beings. As we have noted at the beginning of the chapter, the Christian faith is itself one such universalist account of flourishing life—or, more precisely, it is a quarrelsome family of such accounts of the flourishing life.

Some universalisms are secular, like the philosophy of Nietzsche or the psychology of Freud; others are religious, like Christianity or Islam; still others are somewhere in between, like Buddhism or Confucianism (and perhaps the philosophies of Plato or Spinoza). They all contain what their adherents consider to be universally valid claims about (1) the nature of reality, articulated in mythological, metaphysical, or scientific terms; (2) the self, social relation, and the good; (3) the vision of life that fits both the nature of reality and the character of the self, social relations, and the good; and (4) the proper means of access to the truth of claims 1–3, which endows them with validity.

Even the "soft relativism" so popular in some circles is a universalism, though it may not appear so on first sight. What could the idea of letting each person do his or her own thing have to do with universal values, especially if he or she is doing so by being, for instance, a follower of the Buddha, Jesus, and Muhammad at the same time and seasoning this homemade brew with insights from experimental psychology?[23] But for the soft relativist, letting each person do his or her own thing without subjecting their values to criticism is a moral obligation rooted in the universal *right* of each person to live their own life as they see fit. Intolerance is the corresponding moral transgression that ought not be tolerated.[24]

Though each universalism makes claims to truth, none is a complete and strictly closed system. All universalisms in fact have partly permeable boundaries. This is true, to a degree, even of various forms of fundamentalism, religious or secular, which insist on being embodiments of the pure, original faith.[25] The fact that each universalism contains a significant set of convictions that overlap more or less with the convictions of other universalisms suggests such permeability. Acquaintance with their histories

23. For contemporary bricolage religiosity see Véronique Altglas, *From Yoga to Kabbalah: Religious Exoticism and the Logics of Bricolage* (New York: Oxford University Press, 2014).

24. Charles Taylor, *Varieties of Religion Today: William James Revisited* (Cambridge, MA: Harvard University Press, 2002), 89.

25. The dogmatic and moral stances of all current fundamentalisms were both initially formulated against the backdrop of a specific set of circumstances very different from those of the original they sought to replicate. They also change in response to changes in those circumstances, even if their detractors would argue that these changes are too slow and too restricted. This is certainly true of American Christian fundamentalism. Reflecting on observing American fundamentalism through decades, George Marsden remarks, "One of the intriguing things about fundamentalism in America is that it has been a moving target. The old-time religion has always been changing, innovative, and in many ways up to date. While its core concerns for proclaiming the Gospel, its fundamental doctrines, its concerns for personal piety, and its militant opposition to liberal theology and to secularizing culture remain largely the same as in the 1920s, its ways of expressing those concerns have gone through several transmutations." George Marsden, *Fundamentalism and American Culture*, new ed. (New York: Oxford University Press, 2006), 231. See also his *Reforming Fundamentalism* (Grand Rapids: Eerdmans, 1987), 252–54, where he describes the gradual reforms within Fuller Theological Seminary, which, having roots in American fundamentalism, pioneered women's ordination and political engagement on behalf of the oppressed.

confirms it: each universalism doesn't just change in response to the situation on "the ground"—such as technological, economic, or political transformations—but also through encounter, including contention, with other universalisms. Each of the three great monotheisms, Judaism, Christianity, and Islam, has been and continues to be shaped by the other two, for example. Despite their particular sources and epistemologies, multiple universalisms are, to a certain degree at least, mutually intelligible, able to criticize one another as well as to learn from one another. In a phrase, they are able to shape one another.

Particularity

All universalisms are *particular*. This may seem like a paradox, but it isn't. It's a consequence of the fact that the human beings who make universal claims about the flourishing life are all creatures of time, space, language, and culture. Although their visions are universal in scope, their spread is restricted; even today's most widely embraced universalism, Christianity, commands the adherence of less than a third of the world's population. Though "transplantable" and able to grow anywhere on the planet, each universalism also always has roots in a given place at a given time. The origins, history, and present reality of all universalisms are spatiotemporally particular.

While we have described them as unities—and they often function as such at the level of global social relations—at local levels of social organization, each religious universalism is in fact concrete and alive, less in large movements and more in the particular lives of small communities and individual adherents. The broad coherence of each universalism emerges not just from the common founding figure or founding text but also from the interaction of its adherents at the individual level. We might imagine the relationship between universalisms, their local rival versions, and the concrete individual expressions of their adherents by way of analogy to the relationship between languages, their dialects, and the idiolects spoken by individuals. At the level of concrete experience, only the idiolects "exist"; dialects and languages are abstractions that emerge from the speech patterns of individuals at the level of idiolect. And yet behavior at the individual level is significantly constrained by the frameworks of mutual intelligibility and convention established by the dialects and languages that emerge. So, too, in the case of contending particular universalisms. Take again Christianity as an example. In a certain sense, "Christianity," the global religion, does not "exist" in concrete experience; only the lived piety of billions of individuals and countless overlapping communities of faith exists.

Since time and space inescapably mark universalisms, they are mutable and in fact are always changing, as we noted earlier in the discussion of their permeability: doctrines develop and moral sensibilities shift; practices change, rituals undergo transformations in meaning if not in form. At times, change means departure from the original vision and the beginning of something new, perhaps even incompatible with the original vision (according to some, as when Christianity emerged out of Judaism). At other times, change is a requirement of faithfulness to the original vision under new circumstances (according to some, as when Martin Luther started the Reformation of Latin Christendom). Mostly the disputes about whether the case was one of departure or faithfulness remain unresolved, and change continues within each.

The particularity of universalisms entails a clear rejection of any claim they might make to absoluteness. They make universal claims, but their particularity rules out any one of them being absolute. For illustration, take the case of the Christian faith, a religion that has on occasion been deemed absolute.[26] Christianity

26. On the debate about the "absoluteness of Christianity," see G. W. F. Hegel's *Lectures in Philosophy of Religion*, trans. R. F. Brown et al. (Berkeley: University of California Press, 1984–87), with his ideas of the Absolute coming to consciousness and expressing itself fully in the consummate religion, as well as Ernst Troeltsch's *Absoluteness of Christianity and the History of Religions*, trans. David Reig (Louisville: Westminster John Knox, 2006), in which he contests the claim that Christianity is an absolute religion in part by tracing its historical development in response to various cultural settings.

cannot be absolute, even or especially if we accept its basic and traditional doctrinal claims to be true. Now both the Word, who is the Second Person of the Trinity, and the Trinity itself are absolute; God is the Absolute. But the Word-become-flesh, the God-man Jesus Christ, is not and cannot be absolute precisely because of his inescapably particular humanity. He was born in one place and at one time (in Nazareth around 4 BC), was a speaker of a particular language (a Galilean dialect of Aramaic, and possibly Greek), was steeped in one religious tradition (Judaism) and shaped by a particular hybrid culture (the Jewish, Roman, and Greek culture of Galilee). Even less so should we ascribe absoluteness to any subsequent form of the Christian faith. As the day of Pentecost indicates, from its very inception and expressing in its own way the particularity of Jesus Christ, the church speaks many languages. Moreover, as we noted earlier, Christians, including Christian theologians, can know only in part, never exhaustively and never with indubitable certainty—in a word, never absolutely.[27]

Contention

Finally, the diverse universalisms aren't merely sitting next to one another like different flavors of ice cream in the shop freezer. Each is a claimant not just to our preference but to our allegiance, some even to our ultimate allegiance. Each is a *contending* candidate for deep convictions orienting our entire lives, grounding our values and shaping our preferences. By "contending" we mean that universalisms are always (implicitly, at least) both contesting one another intellectually and jostling with one another for power in a common space.[28] After all, to formulate a vision of the

27. Islam might be the only religion whose deep convictions, according to a historically prevalent view among the Sunni majority, justifies a self-understanding as an absolute religion. The claim is that the Qur'an was not created but is co-eternal with God. "Koran," in *The New Encyclopedia of Islam*, ed. Cyril Glassé, rev. ed. (Walnut Creek, CA: AltaMira, 2001), 267–68.

28. Our vision for public space—including the university—as a site for the contending of multiple particular universalisms is consonant with the vision advanced in Kathryn Tanner, "Theology and Cultural Contest in the University," in

flourishing life with a claim to truth is to offer an alternative table of values and therefore to contest, at least in part, other already existing tables of value. Similarly, to live a vision of the flourishing life is to take social space and exert social influence where other actors are already present and doing the same. How much space a person or a community will take and in what way they will exert influence will differ, but the *fact* of filling a space and exerting influence will remain.

That said, contending universalisms are not necessarily "violent." Contending for a given truth claim *can* lead to violence, but it need not. Most universalisms have their own, more or less effective, internal ways of controlling the violence that they might generate—for example, commitments to impartiality (e.g., in classical Utilitarianism), to justice (e.g., in Islam), to compassion (e.g., in Buddhism), and the like. In fact, given the permeability, alterability, and historicity of universalisms, contending, if responsibly done, can lead to mutual learning and result in social compromise and conviviality.

Responsible contending will not happen without intentional effort. Managing contending universalisms is a central challenge of our pluralistic age. There is a political side to this challenge: fostering political societies that understand themselves as pluralistic with legal arrangements and cultural sensibilities that permit and encourage each person and each community to speak and contend in the public square, unless its proponents advocate and engage in violence. To meet the challenge, we need two things: (1) political philosophies that are open to all overarching interpretations of life and (2) articulations of overarching interpretations of life—religious ones as well as secular ones—that are open to pluralistic kinds of political and legal arrangements.[29]

There is also a pedagogical side to the challenge of managing contending universalisms in pluralistic settings. We need to foster

---

Religious Studies, Theology, and the University: Conflicting Maps, Changing Terrain, ed. Linell E. Cady and Delwin Brown (Albany: SUNY Press, 2002), 199–212.

29. On the dual approach to managing contending particular universalisms politically, see Volf, *Flourishing*, 97–194.

educational institutions that consider it part of their responsibility to facilitate critical discussion and appropriation of visions of flourishing life, including the claims they make on our self-understanding, our aspirations, and our images of a desirable future for the world. Such educational institutions will need to see themselves as sites of truth-seeking critical conversation and personal transformation, equipping students to do the difficult work of evaluating the truth claims of multiple contending particular universalisms and contending in a responsible give-and-take on behalf of the universalism they embrace.[30]

Can Christian faith not just exist as one such contending particular universalism but articulate itself theologically so as to positively contribute to managing the relations between contending particular universalisms in pluralistic societies? Or must Christian theology and the Christian faith be managed from the outside because they are inherently coercive, unfit for peace with others in pluralistic societies?

Christian Faith and Violence

Over the course of Christianity's almost-twenty-centuries-long history, Christians have suffered persecution, they have done the persecuting, and they have both suffered and persecuted on massive scales. Are these two contrary experiences simply two sides of the same violent coin that Christian faith is by its very nature? Did Christians absorb the harsh intolerance they encountered but let it fester itself into their own intolerant mind set and practice, such that the "intolerance of victims" then morphed into "intolerance of perpetrators" when the opportunity arose?[31] Did Christians'

30. This pedagogical side of the task of managing contending universalisms assumes educational settings that welcome—at least provisionally—the various rationalities and epistemologies that contending particular universalisms bring with them, rather than insisting on a particular set of acceptable methodologies and approaches to rationality.

31. On the categories of negative or passive intolerance of victims and positive or active intolerance of perpetrators, see Assmann, *Price of Monotheism*, 20–21.

own cruel intolerance light and fuel the intolerance of those who were its targets? There are many examples of both. But the key question is whether the Christian faith has resources, internal to its account of the flourishing life, to contend intellectually and socially with other universalisms without becoming a source of violence. We will argue that it does. So why does it have a history of active intolerance? Under what conditions did Christian theologians shove these resources aside and proceeded to legitimize intolerance, persecution, and violence?

In *Does Christianity Cause War?* David Martin, a sociologist, proposed how, in a given setting, various elements of an account of the Christian faith come to form a unity—how they get "improvised," to borrow the image we will use below—and offered an explanation of the conditions under which Christian faith gets formulated to legitimize violence. We can look at the Christian faith, he suggested, as "a specific repertoire of linked motifs, internally articulated in a distinctive manner, and giving rise to characteristic explorations, but rendered recognizable by some sort of reference back to the New Testament and 'primitive tradition.'"[32] Depending on the setting and guiding interests, Christians—including theologians—push some motifs into the background, play up others, and orchestrate them with various degrees of consonance or dissonance with each other and with the setting, all the while striving to be faithful to the New Testament and primitive traditions.

There are circumstances, Martin argues, under which Christian faith is likely to be configured to legitimize violence. They occur "when religion becomes virtually coextensive with society and thus with the dynamics of power, violence, control, cohesion, and marking of boundaries."[33] This is what happened to Christianity when it became the dominant religion of the empire.[34] As a result, the Christian account of political rule, for instance, started drawing more on the figure of King David, a monarch of questionable

---

32. David Martin, *Does Christianity Cause War?* (Oxford: Oxford University Press, 1997), 32.
33. Martin, *Does Christianity Cause War?*, 134.
34. See Volf, *Flourishing*, 186–90.

moral standing and a warrior, than on Jesus Christ, the Messiah whose glory was manifest not just in resurrection and exaltation but also, and perhaps above all, in his "greatest humiliation," as Johann Sebastian Bach, leaning on the Gospel of John (17:1), puts it in the opening chorus of his St. John Passion. Under those same circumstances also, Tertullian's "it is unjust to compel freemen against their will" in matters of religion could give way to Augustine's "compel them to come in."[35]

It is clearly possible to legitimize violence with the help of the Christian faith. Many great theologians have done so (though some would contest that the deployment of power they legitimized is properly described as "violence"). It is also possible, with arguments we consider wrong, to advocate for an antipluralist, unitary Christian state whose laws are to be aligned with God's revealed will. At the same time, there are compelling pluralistic alternatives, which we would argue are more faithful to Jesus Christ, a marginal Jew, and to the whole New Testament.

Pillars of a Pluralistic Social Vision

What are some key elements of a Christian account of the flourishing life that allow those who embrace it to live in peace and pursue common good in pluralistic settings, and to do so not only notwithstanding its claim to be true for every human and the entire world, but also largely because of it?

First, *trinitarian monotheism*. Monotheism, some people contend, is the most violent form of religion (all religions supposedly being violent on account of their irrationality). The oneness of God, the extreme version of the story goes, stands for universal sameness.[36] But the one God is the source not just of the unity of the world but also of all the stunning diversity in it. Since,

35. Tertullian, *Ad Scapulum II*, quoted in John R. Bowlin, "Tolerance among the Fathers," *Journal of the Society of Christian Ethics* 26, no. 1 (2006): 18; Augustine, *Letter 93 to Vincentius*, §5.

36. See Regina Schwartz, *The Curse of Cain: The Violent Legacy of Monotheism* (Chicago: University of Chicago Press, 1997), 15–16.

for Christians, the one God is the Holy Trinity, God is internally differentiated. Difference is not secondary, subsequent to unity; difference is equiprimordial with unity.[37]

Second, the *God of unconditional love*. God is not a mere omnipotent force. Neither is God a mere universal lawgiver. The central attribute of God is unconditional love. As a creator, God loves unconditionally. God brings all creatures into being and keeps them in being. God's power doesn't come to creatures first from outside as either supporting or constraining force; in relation to creatures, it is first of all the power of their being, establishing their identities. As ruler and redeemer, too, God loves unconditionally. God's law is not the arbitrary imposition of a ruler hungry for power and glory; God is always already the Most High with or without human obedience; God's law is but a mode of God's love. Even when humans fail to live according to the law of love, God seeks to mend the world and bring it to its intended fullness so it can become what God created it to be: our home and God's home in one.[38]

Third, *Jesus Christ, the light of the world*. Jesus Christ, the Gospel of John claims, is the incarnate Word who was at the beginning with God and through whom "all things came into being" and who is "the light of all people" (John 1:3–4). All light and all truth, whether possessed by Christians or non-Christians, is the light of the Word and therefore Christ's light. This too is the consequence of monotheism: not just that the truth about flourishing life that Christ proclaimed is for all people, but also that in virtue of Christ all people always already possess some of that truth, that they have what Justin Martyr famously called "seeds

37. See Miroslav Volf, "'The Trinity Is Our Social Program': The Doctrine of the Trinity and the Shape of Social Engagement," *Modern Theology* 14, no. 3 (July 1998): 409; Volf, "Being as God Is: Trinity and Generosity," in *God's Life in Trinity*, ed. Miroslav Volf and Michael Welker (Minneapolis: Fortress, 2006), 3–12.

38. On creation and the entire history of salvation as an expression of God's unconditional love, which, in an important sense, always creates "out of nothing," see Luther, "The Magnificat," in *Luther's Works* (St. Louis: Concordia, 1956), 21:299–300.

of the Word."[39] It cannot be otherwise: if the Word is the creator of everything, all genuine insights derive from the God who was in Jesus Christ. All truth sought and found anywhere takes us, ultimately, to Christ as its origin.

Fourth, *distinction between God's rule and human rule.* Monotheism, at least as Christians have understood it, implies two categorically distinct, though related realms, transcendent and mundane, with the absolute primacy given to the transcendent. It follows that religion (allegiance to God) is a distinct, though not entirely separate, "cultural system" from politics (allegiance to a particular state). The entry of the Christian faith into a political space always pluralizes that space: an individual or a community emerges whose primary allegiance is to the God of Jesus Christ rather than to the community itself, its rulers, or any source of legitimacy they may invoke.[40] The Christian church is (or at any rate ought to understand itself as) a loose international network of communities whose primary allegiance isn't to the states of which they are citizens or to some yet-to-be-created global super-state but to the one God of all people. Political pluralism and transnationalism fit well with the Christian vision of flourishing life.

Fifth, the *moral equality of all human beings.* God made all human beings in God's image, and Christ came to announce the universal rule of a God whose chief commands are to love God and neighbor, including the enemy. All people have equal dignity; all have the same rights and the same moral obligations; all have fallen short of those obligations. There are no moral outsiders according to the Christian faith.

Sixth, *freedom of religion and areligion.* The call of Jesus Christ "Come, follow me!" presumes that an individual who hears it is free to follow or not. From the earliest beginnings, it was clear that faith is either embraced freely or not at all: one *believes with*

39. Justin Martyr, *First Apology* §32.
40. See Nicholas Wolterstorff, *The Mighty and the Almighty: An Essay in Political Theology* (Cambridge: Cambridge University Press, 2012), 121–22.

the heart,[41] which is to say not by outward conformity to ambient influences or in reaction to outside dictates backed by overwhelming force but with the very core of one's being. Behind the stress on embracing faith freely lies the conviction that every person has the responsibility for the basic direction of his or her life.

These six principles are foundational to the Christian faith, we would argue. If we embrace them, we will be able, *because of* rather than *despite* our Christian convictions, both to nurture a culture of respect in pluralistic societies and to help craft political regimes of respect that open up the space for particular universalisms to dispute with each other intellectually in search of truth and to struggle for social space without employing violence.

Improvisations

In the previous section, we discussed the possible threat that Christian claims to truth pose to social peace. In this section, we take up the concern that Christian universalism poses an equally dire threat to the *individuality* of persons. The idea that a vision of life can be true for every human being everywhere seems to transgress against the ideal of authenticity, a pervasive contemporary way of thinking about the kind of life that is good for us to live. The authenticity in question can be individual: each person is unique, and I can flourish only by living in sync with who I am deep down, something I can only find out on my own by identifying my capacities and listening to my yearnings. Alternatively, authenticity can be communal, a view many advocate especially about indigenous cultures before colonial conquests: each culture is unique and members of a cultural group can flourish only when their individual lives are attuned to deep convictions and abiding practices of the group.[42] In many cases, these

41. An implication of Rom. 10:10.
42. For the critique of Christian missionaries "stealing" the culture from the people to whom they brought the faith, especially in the trail of colonial conquests,

two forms of authenticity interweave: social beings that we are, we find our "true self" while discovering "who we are" culturally and socially.[43]

Can a Christian vision of flourishing accommodate cultural differences and individual uniqueness? Resting as it does on the convictions that all humans are created in the image of God and that Jesus Christ is the key to human flourishing, must it not squeeze all humans into a single mold, treating them as identical exemplars of generic humanity? The short response: no, it does not. To the extent that a Christian vision of flourishing creates cookie-cutter people, it denies two of its own key convictions. The first is this: human beings are not individual instances of some transtemporal and transspatial human essence but bodily beings and language speakers, and therefore creatures of time, place, and culture. The second conviction is this: no life can, ultimately, be genuinely good if a person wears it as an ill-fitting boot rather than as a well-tailored shirt, if it is the law imposed on them rather than inscribed into their very being.[44] But can the Christian vision of flourishing live up to these convictions? How can a universal faith honor the individual particularities of culturally situated, bodily beings living in the flow of time?

see George E. Tinker, *Missionary Conquest: The Gospel and Native American Cultural Genocide* (Minneapolis: Fortress, 1993).

For a missiological discussion of enculturation, analogous to the Word's incarnation and the Spirit's speaking many languages, see Kwame Bediako, "Biblical Exegesis in the African Context—the Factor and Impact of the Translated Scriptures," *Journal of African Christian Thought* 6 (2003): 15–23; Kwame Bediako, *Theology and Identity: The Impact of Culture upon Christian Thought in the Second Century and in Modern Africa* (Oxford: Regnum, 1992); Andrew F. Walls, *The Missionary Movement in Christian History: Studies in the Transmission of Faith* (Maryknoll, NY: Orbis Books, 1996).

43. Disney's *Moana* displays vividly such dialogical navigation of individual and communal authenticity. Moana discovers that her own personal call away from the village and out onto the open ocean is in fact a call to *return* her people to who they once were. The film's climactic declaration, "I am Moana," is the individual-level echo and consequence of the earlier, and at first private, discovery of the communal vocation: "We were voyagers."

44. On the biblical image of the law being inscribed on the heart, see Jer. 31:33; Heb. 10:16.

We have argued earlier that Christ's kind of life—the goal toward which he was striving and how he did the striving—continues in the community of Christ, the church, through the power of the Spirit. The same Spirit that came to rest on Jesus at the beginning of his ministry came to rest on the church at the beginning of its history. As various New Testament texts suggest, the Spirit is the divine "particularizer." At the birth of the church, the Spirit descended on gathered disciples, and they each spoke in different languages, a clear enactment of the culturally differentiated character of the newborn church.[45] Similarly, in the single local church, the body of Christ in a given place and at a given time, the Spirit gives diverse gifts to its members, each gift a particular way for a unique person to live the life of Christ and continue the mission of Christ.[46] After Christ's ascension his disciples needed to continue to be led into truth; it did not suffice for them to have given allegiance to Christ, who is the "truth." The indwelling Spirit of Christ makes people able to see how the one truth of Christ looks and feels for diverse people at different stages of their lives who live in diverse settings so that they can live "in the truth" (2 John 1). Human life, as all life, is always particular. The Spirit, who, in the words of the Nicene Creed, is the "giver of life," tailors that which was designed for all humans to fit each individual.

Musical improvisation offers a helpful way to think about the relation between the universal vision of life and its particular enactments.[47] Jazz improvisation, for instance, might at first appear

45. See Miroslav Volf, *Exclusion and Embrace: A Theological Exploration of Identity, Otherness, and Reconciliation* (Nashville: Abingdon, 1996), 173–77. See also Willie James Jennings, *Acts,* Belief: A Theological Commentary on the Bible (Louisville: Westminster John Knox, 2017), 28.

46. See 1 Cor. 12:4–31. Cf. also Miroslav Volf, *Work in the Spirit: Toward a Theology of Work* (New York: Oxford University Press, 1991).

47. For the language of improvisation in describing the Christian theological task, see Willie James Jennings, *The Christian Imagination: Theology and the Origins of Race* (New Haven: Yale University Press, 2010), 280–82; Willie James Jennings, "Embodying the Artistic Spirit and the Prophetic Arts," *Literature & Theology* 30, no. 1 (September 2016): 1–9. For the language of improvisation to describe Christian life, see David Ford, *The Drama of Living: Becoming Wise in the Spirit* (Grand Rapids: Brazos, 2014).

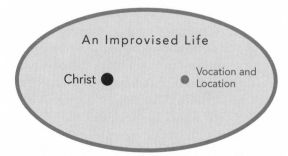

Figure 4.1 The Christian life is improvised in light of the life of Christ and our spatiotemporal, cultural, and vocational particularity. These two generative poles are represented here by the two foci of each ellipse. The ellipse represents the individual life improvised in light of these two foci.

to be wholly free, unfettered, and unstructured. In reality, there is a dynamic relationship between the improvisation itself and what we might call an "improvisational structure." The structure places boundaries on the freedom of those who play within it, and by doing so it also makes free play possible and meaningful. In jazz, the harmonic and rhythmic structures of genre (e.g., "blues"), form (e.g., "12-bar blues"), and tune (e.g., "Blue Monk") place such constraints on those who would improvise "over" it or, perhaps better, "within" it.[48] While improvisation is inexhaustible—it is always possible to improvise a novel solo within a given tune—improvisation is not a matter of "anything goes." As many a student of jazz has experienced firsthand, one can do it incorrectly.

Similarly, visions of flourishing serve as structured constraints within which human lives are improvised. At times, the tonality of our lives clashes with the tonality of the vision into which we're living, and we are brought up short, called to repent. And yet this

48. Paul Berliner, *Thinking in Jazz: The Infinite Art of Improvisation* (Chicago: University of Chicago Press, 1994), 63–94. Craig Calhoun compares the structures within which jazz musicians improvise to Pierre Bourdieu's concept of *habitus*. "Pierre Bourdieu," in *The Wiley-Blackwell Companion to Major Social Theorists*, vol. 2, *Contemporary Social Theorists*, ed. George Ritzer and Jeffrey Stepnisky (Malden, MA: Blackwell, 2011).

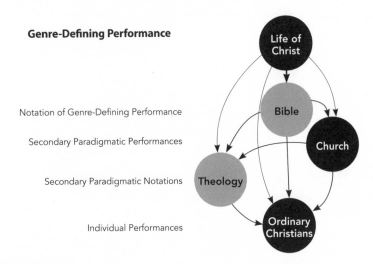

Genre-Defining Performance

Notation of Genre-Defining Performance

Secondary Paradigmatic Performances

Secondary Paradigmatic Notations

Individual Performances

Figure 4.2 Mediation of the normative weight of the life of Christ on the improvisation of Christian lives.

constraint is not only negative. In fact, it is primarily enabling and generative. The same vision of flourishing that constrains provides, for instance, a horizon of significance against which our free choices are meaningful, rescuing us from the nagging demon of arbitrariness.[49]

The normative vision of flourishing comes from the life of Christ, a particular life itself lived by the power of the Spirit within and in productive tension with a previously existing vision of flourishing (largely, the Second Temple Judaism of Roman Palestine). On our musical analogy (which we're quickly stretching to its breaking point!), we could imagine Christ's life as a "genre-defining performance," a concrete enactment that opens up a sufficiently new set of compositional and improvisational possibilities that it is recognized (usually only retrospectively) to hold within itself an entire new genre. In an analogous way—keeping in mind that we are shifting from the domain of aesthetic to that

49. On authenticity and "horizons of significance," see Charles Taylor, *Ethics of Authenticity* (Cambridge, MA: Harvard University Press, 1992), 37–69.

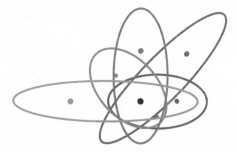

Figure 4.3 Multiple, different improvised Christian lives. The central focus shared by each ellipse represents the shared normative influence of the life of Christ, and the focus unique to each ellipse represents the unique set of spatiotemporal, cultural, and vocational particularities that also shape each improvisation. Each ellipse here represents an equally valid improvisation, differing based on the particular circumstances in which individuals or communities are improvising their lives.

of ultimate concern—the life of Christ is particular and yet universally normative.

Now, we don't have a "recording" of the "performance" of Christ's life. Rather, biblical writers, chiefly the evangelists but also the apostles through whom we first learn about Christ, take up Christ's performance by already beginning to translate Christ's concrete enactment of the universal truth of our existence for culturally distinct communities of their time. The task of Christian theologians is analogous to that of the evangelists and the apostles: building on their "performance" and within the space opened up and structured by Christ, we improvise a universal vision of flourishing for a particular time and place. That's how we may think of the work of Augustine, Maximus the Confessor, and Luther or, closer in our time, the work of C. S. Lewis, Howard Thurman, Jürgen Moltmann, Gustavo Gutiérrez, or Kathryn Tanner. And that's how we may think of each Christian's life, improvised either through a direct reading of the evangelists and apostles or mediated through the work of some theologian.[50]

50. As we do this work of improvisation, sensitive to our contexts—which is to say, to our neighbors—we will discover possibilities latent in the life of Christ that were not yet visible in scriptural sources. This, too, is a feature of improvisation

As we, ordinary Christians and theologians, discern the vision of flourishing opened to us in the life of Christ, we ought to look to the particular enactments of Christian life that have been and are being crafted around us. Discerning Christianly will mean above all looking for a profound resonance with the life of Christ in Scripture and also with the possibilities for Christian life held in trust among the great cloud of witnesses from past and present. We should search them out, learn to hear in them the voice of the author of the tune, and imaginatively improvise the next few bars.

---

itself. Exploring the boundaries of what is possible, an imaginative improvisation can reveal potentialities not yet realized within a given structure, expanding the structure through revealing its capaciousness. Contributing to the developing improvisational tradition, each such successful realization of latent possibilities lays particular responsibilities on improvisations that follow, imbuing newly discovered features with a certain normative weight. In jazz, one might think of the "turn-arounds" at the end of harmonic patterns or "tritone substitutions." In Christian theology, one might think of the developments like the doctrine of the Trinity or of salvation by grace alone, or certain ecclesial or domestic liturgies.

5

Lives of Theologians

with Justin Crisp

─────────── **Search for Truth, Life in Truth** ───────────

The main argument of this book is that theology ought to serve the kind of flourishing of life exemplified in the story of Jesus Christ and sketched in the great promise of the entire world becoming God's home. Put simply and in the phrase of one of theology's most influential practitioners, Christian theology is faith seeking understanding.[1] But faith for us is not merely a set of beliefs, not even only personal trust supported by a set of convictions. It is an

1. Anselm, *Proslogion*, prooemium (preface), in *Opera Omnia*, vol. 1, ed. F. S. Schmitt (Edinburgh: Thomas Nelson and Sons, 1940–61), 95. The phrase has origins in the prophet Isaiah (7:9) and the apostle Paul: "We . . . believe, and so we speak" (2 Cor. 4:13). The connection between the two verses seems odd in contemporary translations. The Septuagint, however, translates Isa. 7:9 with the same terms as those in Matt. 13:14. The parallel was hence quite obvious for Anselm and his predecessor Augustine, but our translations, based more closely on the best available Hebrew manuscripts, do not convey this. See Gareth Matthews, "Anselm, Augustine, and Platonism," in *The Cambridge Companion to*

entire way of life. Theology is *a way of life seeking understanding.* More precisely, it is one dimension of that way of life.[2]

To argue that theology is a way of life seeking understanding is to raise the question of the relation between the way of life theologians live and the way of life they articulate and commend. Beyond interest in the subject matter, professional commitment to the scientific method, and the possession of the requisite skills and discipline to engage in the endeavor, the lives of astrophysicists or of molecular biologists are largely irrelevant to doing astrophysics and microbiology. Is the same true of theologians? Or do the lives of theologians need to align, in some sense at least, with the way of life they seek to articulate? Might they even need to embody that way of life, to "speak the truth in the form of a manifestation of existence," as Michel Foucault approvingly wrote of the Cynics in one of his last lectures?[3]

Theology's earliest practitioners certainly thought so. For figures like Justin Martyr, Clement of Alexandria, Origen, the Cappadocians, Augustine, and Maximus the Confessor, theology, like Christianity itself, was a way of life. They inherited the idea partly from New Testament writers and partly from ancient philosophers, for whom philosophy was, as Pierre Hadot puts it, "a mode of existing-in-the-world, which ha[s] to be practiced at each instance, and the goal of which [is] to transform the whole of the individual's life."[4] Over the centuries, the unity of life and discourse gradually

---

Anselm, ed. Brian Davies and Brian Leftow (Cambridge: Cambridge University Press, 2004), 65–66.

2. Our point here is not primarily that theology of any sort—including academic theology—is a practice rather than "theory," as Kathryn Tanner has compellingly argued in *Theories of Culture: A New Agenda for Theology* (Minneapolis: Fortress, 1997), 72–79. It is that the "intelligence of faith," as a form of sustained reflection (and so a "practice" in the sense Tanner uses it), is also a dimension of a more encompassing practice, which is the way of life or "faith" itself, rather than merely an extrinsic aid or guide to it.

3. Michel Foucault, *The Courage of Truth: The Government of the Self and Others, II; Lectures at the Collège de France, 1983–1984*, ed. Frédéric Gros, trans. Graham Burchell (New York: Picador, 2011), 217.

4. Pierre Hadot, *Philosophy as a Way of Life: Spiritual Exercises from Socrates to Foucault*, ed. Arnold I. Davidson, trans. Michael Chase (Oxford: Blackwell,

broke apart in both philosophy and theology—and mainly to their detriment.[5] Today's theologians pursue their work in the wake of theology's reinvention as "science" in the modern sense. Like their colleagues in the rest of the humanities, many theologians aspire to be engaged in the project of the incremental increase of knowledge following an adjusted form of the same research methods modern sciences utilize (see chap. 2). Search for truth no longer requires the effort to live in the truth.[6]

At every stage of this transformation, many theologians have resisted the fall of theology into "discourse" or "science" only marginally related to the theologian's own life of faith. Bernard of Clairvaux did so in the Middle Ages: he rooted his theology in "the book of our own experience" and, insisting that knowledge is incomplete if not joined to love, echoed Paul's criticism of "the knowledge that gives self-importance."[7] As we will explore later in this chapter, Martin Luther did so during the Reformation: only a person radically transformed by God, as a rule through suffering, can become a theologian of the cross and have access to proper knowledge of God and of the self, which for Luther is the subject matter of theology.[8] Gustavo Gutiérrez and Katie Geneva Cannon did so in the second half of the twentieth century.

1995). Cf. Augustine, *Contra Julianum* 4.14.72. See also Jean Leclercq, *The Love of Learning and the Desire for God: A Study of Monastic Culture*, trans. Catherine Misrahi (New York: Fordham University Press, 1961), 99–102.

5. For these genealogies, see, e.g., Hadot, *Philosophy as a Way of Life*, 268–71; Foucault, *Courage of Truth*, 235–37; Hans Urs von Balthasar, "Theology and Sanctity," in *Explorations in Theology*, vol. 1, trans. A. V. Littledale with Alexander Dru (San Francisco: Ignatius, 1989), 181–92.

6. See, e.g., the efforts of Friedrich Schleiermacher, *Brief Outline to Theology as a Field of Study*, 3rd ed., trans. Terrence N. Tice (Louisville: Westminster John Knox, 2011), §§1–13. See also David Kelsey, *To Understand God Truly: What's Theological about a Theological School?* (Louisville: Westminster John Knox, 1992), 86–92.

7. See Bernard of Clairvaux, *On the Song of Songs I*, trans. Kilian Walsh, vol. 2 of *The Works of Bernard of Clairvaux* (Kalamazoo, MI: Cistercian Publications, 1971), 16, 48–49; Bernard alludes to 1 Cor. 8:1: "Knowledge puffs up, but love builds up." See also Leclercq, *Love of Learning*, 204–9.

8. See Gerhard O. Forde, *On Being a Theologian of the Cross: Reflections on Luther's Heidelberg Disputation, 1518* (Grand Rapids: Eerdmans, 1997).

For Gutiérrez and other theologians of liberation, theologians are "organic intellectuals"; they can do theology rightly only by living the preferential option for the poor. Cannon and other womanist theologians ground their theology in insights born of black women's experience of the intersecting oppressions of race, class, and gender.[9] Rowan Williams and Sarah Coakley have done so in their own ways as well, Williams by conceiving of apophasis as an "attitude" cultivated by the theologian, which properly disposes her to the unknowable object of her discourse (God) and Coakley by making the "deepening practices" of contemplative prayer central to theological method.[10]

This short and somewhat arbitrary sample illustrates a rich and diverse tradition. In our own way, we align ourselves with it. They and we hark back to the church fathers and, as we shall argue below, to the first of the Christian theologians, the apostle Paul. Our thesis is simple and controversial: *execution of the central theological task requires a certain kind of affinity between the life the theologian seeks to articulate and the life the theologian seeks to lead.* Put succinctly in the words of Jürgen Moltmann to a group of scholars discussing an earlier version of this chapter: without theological life, there is no proper theological work.

Our thesis assumes a distinction between the *primary* vision of the flourishing life—what is sometimes called "the gospel" and what we have, using a musical analogy, termed the "genre-defining performance" of the Christian vision of flourishing (see chap. 4)—and subsequent articulations of this vision, the many *secondary* visions of the flourishing life, which improvise in the

9. See Gustavo Gutiérrez, "Liberation Praxis and Christian Faith," in *The Power of the Poor in History*, trans. Robert R. Barr (Maryknoll, NY: Orbis, 1983), 55–61; Katie Geneva Cannon, *Katie's Canon: Womanism and the Soul of the Black Community* (New York: Continuum, 1995), 124–27.

10. See Rowan Williams, *Wrestling with Angels: Conversations in Modern Theology*, ed. Mike Higton (Grand Rapids: Eerdmans, 2007), 1–2; Rowan Williams, "Theological Integrity," in *On Christian Theology* (Oxford: Blackwell, 2000); Sarah Coakley, "Deepening Practices: Perspectives from Ascetical and Mystical Theology," in *Practicing Theology: Beliefs and Practices in Christian Life*, ed. Miroslav Volf and Dorothy C. Bass (Grand Rapids: Eerdmans, 2002).

genre defined by the gospel. No doubt, secondary visions are the filters through which we inevitably see the primary vision, but such filtering does not cancel the distinction. Fidelity to the primary vision always remains the most important criterion for the adequacy of the secondary visions. For our secondary visions to align with the primary one, theologians need to seek to align our lives with the primary vision—as we understand it. The desire for alignment and the labor of faithful articulation, each influencing the other, create a virtuous cycle that makes the movement of responsible theological improvisation possible.

In this chapter we will argue, first, that an affinity between theologians' lives and the basic vision of the true life that they seek to articulate is a condition of the adequacy of their thought. Second, we will contend that the nature of that affinity is not strict correspondence between the theologian's life and a Christian vision of the true life but rather *striving* for congruence between the two. Third, we will explore the nature of a cycle—virtuous and vicious—between reasoned theological articulations and theologians' lives. We will conclude by identifying key intellectual virtues requisite for doing theological work well. But first, a disclaimer.

In arguing for the affinity between the life theologians seek to articulate and the life they seek to lead, we are, obviously, not trying to compel anyone because of their job title or institutional affiliation to be or become a "theologian" in the robust sense that we articulate here. Neither do we—nor would we—advocate that theological institutions rid themselves of "nontheologians." We *are*, however, extending a call; we are *commending* a way of life and a style of thought to any who would dare to embrace it, be they systematicians, ethicists, homileticians, historians, biblical scholars, or what have you. One can acquire any of these titles today without living as a theologian or doing a theologian's work in the sense we advocate. Still, there is no subfield in which theology as we understand it cannot be, or ought not to be, pursued. Indeed, a theological faculty will fully flourish only with scholars across all these subfields working together *as theologians*. Likewise, theologians will only flourish if they are hospitable toward the research

119

of scholars working as modern academic specialists, a style of thought indispensable to the work of theology as we understand it.

Affinity between Life and Thought

The first and obvious reason for affinity between theologians' lives and visions arises out of a concern for *credibility*. Christian visions of a flourishing life, like all major competing visions, whether religious or secular, are visions of the true life and are therefore of universal import. In broad contours, they sketch the truth of every person's life, and that includes the lives of theologians themselves. A Christian vision of true life is therefore always also a vision of the theologian's life and the theologian's world.[11] It would be incongruous for theologians to articulate and commend as *true* a life that they themselves had no aspiration of embracing. They would then be a bit like a nutritionist who won't eat her fruits and vegetables while urging her patients to do so.

Our main concern in this chapter is with a second, less obvious but more important, reason for the need for affinity between theologians' lived lives and the visions they seek to articulate. Misalignment between lives and visions doesn't just diminish the credibility of theologians; it is prone to undermine the *veracity* of their work because it *hinders their ability to adequately perceive and articulate* these visions. This is the core of our thesis and the part likely to raise eyebrows—even in the weak form in which we advocate it. "Weak," we say, because we will argue (1) that living a certain kind of life doesn't determine the perception and articulation of visions, but only *exerts significant pressure* on them, and (2) that theologians need not perfectly live out the vision they are seeking to articulate (which, as a matter of fact, they cannot), but must only strive to do so. Still, the claim is contestable, seeming

11. On biblical texts being about their readers, see Miroslav Volf, *Captive to the Word of God: Engaging the Scriptures for Contemporary Theological Reflection* (Grand Rapids: Eerdmans, 2010), 20–22.

to make theology into a subjective, elitist, and esoteric endeavor. What justifies it?

Reasons and the Orientation of the Self

Reasons are insufficient to identify a vision of flourishing as good or to keep holding on to it in the course of our lives. Though arguments matter when it comes to such a vision—they can alert us to internal inconsistencies or situational inadequacies of a vision, for instance—they don't suffice; a vision is underdetermined by arguments.[12] Willingness to embrace a vision of the good life and hold on to it is crucially tied to the values with which we identify and to the kind of selves we desire to be. As Charles Taylor has argued, when we embrace a new vision of life, we undergo a major transvaluation of values; we become "new" persons.

For *becoming* a new person, a leap of intuitive self-identification of the old self with what it is to become is indispensable.[13] But the good, flourishing life is not just a matter of becoming a new

---

12. Take, for example, Friedrich Nietzsche's account of the "good life." In *The Anti-Christ*, he explains that his central concern is "what type of human . . . should be *willed*." He insists that to answer this most fundamental human question we must know answers to questions like the following: What is good? What is bad? What is happiness? (Friedrich Nietzsche, *The Anti-Christ*, in *"The Anti-Christ," "Ecce Homo," "Twilight of the Idols," and Other Writings*, ed. Aaron Ridley and Judith Norman, trans. Judith Norman [New York: Cambridge University Press, 2005], §3, p. 4). All of the most basic human values are in play when we attempt to name the kind of human being we ought to be. That's why arguments do not suffice to motivate the embrace of a vision. When Nietzsche complained that his contemporaries didn't have "ears . . . for [his] truths" (*Ecce Homo*, in *"Anti-Christ," "Ecce Homo,"* §1, p. 100; see also *Anti-Christ*, p. 3), he was not bemoaning their lack of intellectual acuity but their weakness, resentment, and cowardice—their lack of courage to embrace the type of human Nietzsche advocated (Nietzsche, *Ecce Homo*, §3, p. 72). As he undertook his "revaluation of all values" (Nietzsche, *Anti-Christ*, §62, p. 66)—Dionysus versus the Crucified— he fully expected some of his readers to resist becoming the kind of humans he wanted "bred," as he crassly put it (Nietzsche, *Anti-Christ*, §3, p. 4). Similarly, John Stuart Mill, "Utilitarianism," in *"On Liberty," and Other Essays*, ed. John Gray (Oxford: Oxford University Press, 1998), 134.

13. On the process, see Charles Taylor, *The Language Animal: The Full Shape of Human Linguistic Capacity* (Boston: Harvard University Press, 2016), 197–99.

person but of living out the new identity. Living *as* new persons in the flow of time and in a cross-pressured personal and social space in which both the vision and its enactments are questioned and assailed from many sides, every step of the way we must, tacitly at least, both reaffirm the vision and discern how to live it concretely in new situations. Just as reasons, though important, don't suffice to embrace a vision of the good life, so reasons, though even more important, don't suffice to discern how to live it out. Our contention is that an abiding aspirational alignment of the self with the vision and its values is essential as well.

This is a sketch of a general argument for the affinity between the labor of life and the labor of thought, applicable to all—or, at least, most—visions of the good life. When it comes to a specifically Christian vision of the good life, the need for affinity is also rooted in the conviction that there are resistances to the vision and pressures to distort it that do not stem just from divergence of visions and changes in settings but above all from the power of sin to pull us away from the good, to cloud our vision of the good, and to generate justificatory arguments for distorting the good. That's why conversion in the Christian tradition, mostly undertaken with a mixture of good reasons and properly oriented desire, isn't just an event that commences the journey of faith but also a process that accompanies the entirety of it. The temptation of sin, and not just—not even primarily—the need for discernment in the flow time and change of settings, requires that there be affinity between the kind of life theologians aspire to live and the primary vision they seek to articulate.

Reorientation, Transformation, and Access to Truth

Consider how the apostle Paul thought of the relations between reason, desire, and the true life, with regard to both coming to faith and practicing faith. He clearly did not belittle arguments. He was trained "in knowledge," and it mattered to him that his hearers and readers understood this (2 Cor. 11:6). As he saw it, part of his responsibility was to "destroy [the] arguments" of opponents and to "take every thought captive" (10:4–5). Yet he insisted that knowledge and arguments alone could not do the job. Why? Here is how he puts it: "The god of this world"—the tradition-mediated, culturally legitimized, and materially reinforced ways of life, along with their guardians—"has blinded the minds of the unbelievers, to keep them from seeing the light of the gospel of the glory of Christ" (4:4).[14]

The blindness was hardly surprising. Christ crucified and resurrected was the pivot around which Paul's vision of human fullness, values he advocated, and his entire thought revolved. What could be more absurd than the idea of placing a crucified man, even the one who was raised from the dead, at the center of all human aspirations, calling this failed teacher and martyred marginal master the "Lord of glory" (1 Cor. 2:8)?! From the perspective of those who, at the most fundamental level, trusted wisdom, this was bound to appear as imbecilic foolishness, and from the perspective of those who ultimately trusted power, as contemptible weakness (1:18–25). Similarly, those whose "god is the belly" and whose "minds are set on earthly things" were, unsurprisingly, "enemies of the cross of Christ" (Phil. 3:18–19).

In contrast, those who, like Paul, oriented their entire lives toward the crucified and resurrected Jesus Christ (Phil. 3:7–14) had a radically different account of wisdom and power. What ordinarily passes as wisdom and power were, for them, in fact foolish and weak; they believed that the world's wisdom and power along with its recognized sages and powerful rulers were "doomed to perish" (1 Cor. 1:28; 2:6). Similarly, from the perspective of Paul, those who made the belly their god rather than worshiping God as revealed in the crucified Jesus Christ betrayed God and their very selves.[15] To perceive a form of life contrary to our own as truly

14. For Paul, see also 1 Cor. 1:17–2:16.

15. For Paul, the contrast in the ways of life is predominantly stark: foolishness vs. wisdom; weakness vs. power; belly vs. God; the schema of the world vs. the schema of Christ. But the basic point about the alignment of life with the vision stands even when one recognizes that the competing schemas partly overlap and that there are continuities and parallels and not just discontinuities and contrasts.

desirable, to recognize in it the pearl of great price for which we are willing to sell everything, requires more than good vision and hearing, more than reliable information combined with unassailable arguments. It requires a death of the self and its rising again and a resultant shift in seeing and hearing, *a new set of eyes and ears as the organs of a new self.*[16]

Important for Paul was not just a one-time reorientation from one way of life to another, an over-and-done-with dying and rising of the self, a once-and-for-all revolution in the self's entire orientation. That's not how human hearts work in the twilight before the darkness has given way to the daylight (Rom. 13:12), in a world that has become new and yet very much remains old as well (see our chaps. 3 and 6). Even for the new self, transformation is indispensable. "Do not be conformed to this world, but be transformed by the renewing of your minds, so that you may discern what is the will of God—what is good and acceptable and perfect" (12:2). The initial revolution in orientation, the adoption of the new schema of the self and the world, is crucial, but it is just the beginning of a journey and of the process by which the self gets aligned with the new schema: "Keep being transformed," writes Paul, using present passive imperative. As we live in time, and as the time in which we live is filled with tension between the old and the new, transformation must be ongoing, in fact a *growth* out of the old schema and into the new one.

Underpinning the soteriological imperative is an anthropological conviction: the relation of the self to its schema (or its ultimate end) is such that the self can have a particular schema only by actively stretching itself into it. The consequence of both soteriological and anthropological convictions is this: just as in adopting the new

16. In insisting on the affinity between the life people live and the visions of the true life they are ready to embrace, Paul is in line with the teaching of Jesus (Mark 4:12), again with the stress on the beginning of the journey, though with an implicit affirmation of the need for affinity for traveling on the journey as well, for discerning individual steps that need to be made. Jesus himself was, in turn, echoing the Hebrew prophets (Isa. 6:9–10; Jer. 5:21; Ezek. 12:2), who believed that we can "have eyes to see" but not see and "ears to hear" but not hear.

schema blindness is removed and sight is given—or just as new schema and new eyes are given in one act—so the ongoing transformation of the self into the new schema is needed in the day-to-day movement of life so that the person becomes able to discern "what is good and acceptable and perfect."[17] Of course, though crucial, the ongoing transformation is not a sufficient condition of discernment.

This was also Paul's own experience in becoming a follower of Christ and working as a theologian of the church he had once persecuted. The shift in what he considered to be ultimately desirable occurred through a dramatic self-revelation of Christ, a gift of sight and an effectual call to live his entire life into conformity with Christ (Gal. 1:13–17). It shaped his take on the affinity between his life and the content of his theology. He attributed the blindness and deafness to the power of evil and credited the opening of his eyes and ears to the power of God's Spirit. The shift itself was a major reorientation of the self, not as a one-time event but as the beginning of "being transformed" into Christ's image (2 Cor. 3:18). Only those who are and continue to be "spiritual" can—*can*, not necessarily *will*—perceive "spiritual things"; to those who are not, the gifts that God bestows through the crucified Lord of glory will appear as "foolishness" (1 Cor. 2:6–16).[18]

Building on Paul, theologians as different as Gregory of Nazianzus and Martin Luther have insisted that to perceive and articulate true life *as true* there must be an affinity between the eyes and ears

17. We will note in chap. 6 that "perfect" (*teleios*) is an important word for Paul's understanding of flourishing life, describing *both* the eschatological flourishing life *and* its realization in this age.

18. In a certain way, our argument would seem to characterize theological knowledge as esoteric, inaccessible to the uninitiated. Gregory of Nazianzus, for instance, suggests a strong version of this (see Oration 27.3, in *On God and Christ: The Five Theological Orations and Two Letters to Cledonius*, trans. Frederick Williams and Lionel Wickham [Crestwood, NY: St. Vladimir's Seminary Press, 2002], 26–27). Together with Augustine, we want to resist this push. We hope, in fact, to restore to academic theology the character of shared striving in faith seeking understanding that, Augustine thinks, levels the playing field between theologians and their hearers and readers. See John C. Cavadini, "Simplifying Augustine," in *Educating People of Faith: Exploring the History of Jewish and Christian Communities*, ed. John van Engen (Grand Rapids: Eerdmans, 2004), 69–81.

and what they are seeing and hearing.[19] As Michel Foucault, a non-theologian, put it regarding the philosophers of antiquity, so it has been for many Christian theologians through the centuries, and so it is for us: the articulation of the true life requires us to carry out "transformations on [ourselves] in order to have access to the truth."[20]

Collective Pressure, Communal Transformation

As we have formulated it, the demand for affinity between theologians' lived lives and their take on the primary vision they seek to articulate is addressed to them as individuals. That's because each theologian is ultimately responsible for his or her life and work. Like all humans, however, theologians live within social imaginaries and networks of power that exert pressure on their lives and their work: "pre-ontologies," cultural mentalities, economic and political systems, institutions, and more.[21] The apostle Paul invokes the power of "the god of this world" (2 Cor. 4:4) or, as he puts it elsewhere, the "form of this world" (1 Cor. 7:31; cf. Rom. 12:2), and transpersonal Sin (Rom. 6:6)[22] to explain the inability of unbelievers to properly identify what—from the perspective of his gospel—is truly desirable. Correspondingly, transformative renewal of the mind has a *collective* aspect—"be transformed [*metamorphousthe*, pl.] by the renewing of the mind [*noos*, sg.]" (12:2)—just as does the debasing of the mind: "God gave them [pl.] up to a debased mind [sg.]" (1:28).[23]

19. For Gregory of Nazianzus, see Oration 27.2–3, in *On God and Christ*, 25–27. For Martin Luther, see "Heidelberg Disputation," in *Luther's Works* (Philadelphia: Fortress, 1955–86), 31:52–54.

20. Michel Foucault, *The Hermeneutics of the Subject: Lectures at the Collège de France, 1981–1982*, ed. Frédéric Gros, trans. Graham Burchell (New York: Picador, 2005), 15.

21. For such contexts of understanding, see Charles Taylor, *A Secular Age* (Cambridge, MA: Belknap, 2007), 3–4; Taylor, *Modern Social Imaginaries* (Durham, NC: Duke University Press, 2004), 23–30.

22. For an extended account of Sin in this transpersonal or "mythological" sense, see Matthew Croasmun, *The Emergence of Sin: The Cosmic Tyrant in Romans* (New York: Oxford University Press, 2017), 102–39.

23. It is particularly clear in Rom. 1:28 that the singular form of "mind" is intentional and not merely intended to be understood as distributive (that is, as

We can parse out his point in more mundane terms. Over past centuries and through today, rulers of diverse political regimes—whether secular or religious—have regulated what kinds of lives theologians are allowed to live and what kinds of works they can safely produce.[24] Similarly, though more subtly, the market economy exerts pressure on theologians, bending their lives toward certain goods and nudging them to produce marketable work—the kind that will attract tuition-paying students or sell books.[25] Or, we can think of the imperialist and racist mentalities that structure the imagination of whole societies and sweep theologians into conformity, making it difficult for all but the most humanly and spiritually alert to recognize the betrayal of the gospel that these mentalities represent.[26] Finally, let's not forget academic institutions. They have their own way of disciplining theologians, both their desires and the direction of their work.[27] Theological lives often have to be lived against social imaginaries and networks of power.

---

effectively equivalent to the plural, "minds"), as Paul was quite happy to use the grammatical plural for "the desire of their *hearts*" merely four verses earlier (Rom. 1:24, authors' translation).

24. The history of the persecution of theologians is long, from the Roman persecutions that punctuated the church's first centuries (see W. H. C. Frend, *The Early Church* [Philadelphia: Fortress, 1982]), through the intra-Christian political vacillations of the English Reformation in the sixteenth (see Ole Peter Grell, Jonathan I. Israel, and Nicholas Tyacke, eds., *From Persecution to Toleration: The Glorious Revolution and Religion in England* [Oxford: Clarendon, 1991]), up to the repression of Christians during the Cultural Revolution in China in the twentieth (Daniel H. Bays, *A New History of Christianity in China* [Chichester, UK: Wiley-Blackwell, 2012], 92–208).

25. Foucault's reflections on "governmentality" trace how the state and the markets operate on the level of the self's relation to the self. See Michel Foucault, *The Birth of Biopolitics: Lectures at the Collège de France, 1978–1979*, ed. Michel Senellart, trans. Graham Burchell (New York: Macmillan, 2008). See also Kathryn Tanner, "Christianity and the New Spirit of Capitalism," Gifford Lectures, University of Edinburgh, May 2–12, 2016, https://www.giffordlectures.org/lectures/christianity-and-new-spirit-capitalism.

26. See Willie James Jennings, *The Christian Imagination: Theology and the Origins of Race* (New Haven: Yale University Press, 2010); Edward Said, *Orientalism* (New York: Pantheon, 1978).

27. See Keri Day, "Modern Capitalism and Its Discontents: The Practice of Moral Courage in the Theologian's Life," paper presented at a consultation on the

At the same time, social imaginaries and networks of power can also be theologians' allies, making faithful living and responsible work easier. For example, social pluralism—the fact that many ethnic and religious groups have come to coinhabit the same political space—has helped decouple millennia-long alliances of theology with political powers.[28] Similarly, the modern economy has pulled women out of the domestic sphere into "public" life in the world and, though inequality in pay still persists, has helped lend plausibility to aspects of a Christian vision of human equality that remained obscure to many Christians over the centuries.[29] Theologians are responsible for discerning which aspects of their settings to resist or exit and which aspects to build up or celebrate.[30] And for that task, too—no, for that task above all!—they will need to strive to align their lives as individuals and as communities with the primary Christian vision of the true life.

Theologians as Pilgrims

What kind of affinity between theologians' lives and the primary Christian vision of the flourishing life would make it possible to do theological work well? One answer could be: a perfect correspondence. Those whose lives perfectly aligned with Christ's would

future of theology at the Yale Center for Faith and Culture, New Haven, CT, April 1–2, 2016; Maggie Berg and Barbara K. Seeber, *The Slow Professor: Challenging the Culture of Speed in the Academy* (Toronto: University of Toronto Press, 2016).

28. See Miroslav Volf, *Flourishing: Why We Need Religion in a Globalized World* (New Haven: Yale University Press, 2015), 84–87.

29. For women's shift from the domestic to the public sphere in the twentieth century, see Claudia Goldin, "The Quiet Revolution That Transformed Women's Employment, Education, and Family," *American Economic Review* 96, no. 2 (May 2006): 1–21.

30. On the need for such a differentiated stance toward their settings, see Miroslav Volf, *A Public Faith: How Followers of Christ Should Serve the Common Good* (Grand Rapids: Brazos, 2011), 89–97; Miroslav Volf, *Captive to the Word of God: Engaging the Scriptures for Contemporary Theological Reflection* (Grand Rapids: Eerdmans, 2010), 65–90.

then be the only true theologians.[31] But that cannot be right, at least not if we have theology as a specialized practice in view, as we do here.

Should we then perhaps say that only the saints can *potentially* be true theologians? In this case, sanctity would be indispensable but not sufficient. Requisite abilities, calling, and training would be needed as well. The true theologian would then be the person who embraces a calling to the theological task, whose mind is capacious and trained, and whose life is perfectly attuned to Christ's. In a way, this is the *ideal case* of what we are proposing: the kind of life theologians live would manifest the kind of life they articulate, critically examine, and commend, and, inversely, their articulations would express the kind of life they live. This would be a *strict homomorphy* between truly excellent life and proper articulation of a Christian vision of the true life.

But the ideal case is also an impossible one. Theologians are *pilgrims* still on the way to full conformity to Christ and to the world-become-God's-home. Theology is the practice of *pilgrims seeking understanding*—and anyone else who may want to listen. Consequently, we argue for an *affinity*, rather than a strict homomorphy, of theologians' lives with the primary Christian vision of flourishing (always, of course, an affinity with the primary vision *as they understand it*). The character of this affinity follows from the pilgrim condition in which we live. Leaning on the apostle Paul, we can identify two key features of pilgrim affinity.[32]

Proleptic and Ecstatic Living

As pilgrims, we reach the goal of holiness only partly and always in the act of "pressing on to make it our own," as Paul puts it

31. So François-Marie Léthel, *Connaître l'amour du Christ qui surpasse toute connaissance: La Théologie des saints* (Venasque: Editions du Carmel, 1989), 3; cf. Christoph Cardinal Schönborn, *God Sent His Son: A Contemporary Christology* (San Francisco: Ignatius, 2004), 371.

32. Had we drawn Matthew or James, for instance, our account of affinity would have been different, though analogous.

(cf. Phil. 3:12). In the present age, sanctity exists only in the modes of *incompletion* (or of not having "reached the goal" [v. 12]) and of *striving* (or "straining forward to what lies ahead" [v. 13]). Imperfection, along with the awareness of oneself as imperfect, are essential dimensions of sanctity in this sense. Describing his own life and work, Paul writes: "We have this treasure in clay jars" (2 Cor. 4:7). The "treasure" is the true life—more specifically "the light of the gospel of the glory of Christ" that reveals Christ's life to be the true life (2 Cor. 4:4). The "clay jars" are the fragile, limited, temporal, incomplete, inadequate, fallible persons entrusted with this treasure, which includes Paul himself. His holiness was primarily evident in his *striving* to make the life of Christ his own, not in his having reached that goal. Importantly, that striving itself as well as any achievement resulting from it was rooted in the recognition that Jesus Christ has made Paul "his own"; the goal had come to the one who reached out for it in order to make the very act of reaching out possible (Phil. 3:12). The work of Christian theologians requires living a life of striving toward God's home—in oneself and the world—for which acknowledgment of one's abiding fragilities and ineradicable imperfections is indispensable. In a word, the affinity of theologians' life and work can only be *proleptic*.

This affinity should also be *ecstatic*, in the technical sense of having something of one's own outside oneself. In an important sense, neither the life theologians lead nor the vision of the way of life they seek to articulate *belongs* to them. Theologians' lives, like the Christian life more generally, are not endeavors in self-achievement; their transformations are transformations of the self, but they are not mere *self*-transformations. The life they live is Christ's life; as they behold "the glory of the Lord as though reflected in a mirror," the Spirit of God transforms them "into the same image" (2 Cor. 3:18). That's why theologians, though striving to embody the true life, ought not to commend themselves but the true life itself—that is, Christ (cf. 2 Cor. 3:1; 10:12). In sum, an ecstatic and proleptic sort of affinity provides theologians with the "eyes to see" the truth of the gospel.

Proleptic and Ecstatic Articulations

When it comes to true life, the lives of Christians—and there-fore also of theologians—are always lived in the mode of *prolepsis* and *ecstasis*; theological articulations that draw on this kind of life cannot but take on its proleptic and ecstatic character. First, the articulations too are *proleptic*, existing always only in the mode of incompletion and striving. Every single one of them is inad-equate, both true and distorted, striving to express what, to some degree, remains hidden and is visible only "in a mirror, dimly" (1 Cor. 13:12). That isn't only the result of human fallibility, of the effects of sin whose stain remains indelible and whose power remains ineradicable in this life.

It follows also from the nature of human beings and from the main object of theology, God. As to human beings, to be a person is, by definition, to be incomprehensible.[33] What's more, as we have seen in chapter 4, human beings live in the stream of time and al-ways at a given place. Though we, as theologians, are returning to the same river that is the story of God-with-us, both we ourselves and our audiences are diverse and changing.[34] A theological articu-lation can be fruitful in one place at one time but not at that same place at a different time or at a different place at the same time.

As to the object of theology, the One with whom theologians always have to do is the incomprehensible God, whether they re-flect on the goal of Christian life (the world as God's home) or on the journey to the goal (following God-with-us in the power of God's Spirit). For these three reasons—the incomprehensibility of God, the finitude of theologians and their communities, and

33. We are opaque to ourselves, both knowing and unknowing ourselves—or, in Paul's terms, our spirit knowing what is in us (1 Cor. 2:11) and yet always failing to search deeply enough and express adequately what is in us (cf. Rom. 8:26–27). We are doubly opaque to other human beings and yet also differently known to them as well, whether they are psychologists or theologians or anyone else.

34. See Volf, *Captive to the Word of God*, 26–27. See also Williams, *On Chris-tian Theology*, 3–15; Rowan Williams, "Making Moral Decisions," in *The Cam-bridge Companion to Christian Ethics*, ed. Robin Gill (Cambridge: Cambridge University Press, 2001), 8–11.

their sinfulness—all articulations of the true life are inadequate, incomplete, and straining forward toward the goal.

Second, theologians' articulations ought to be *ecstatic*, again in the technical sense of having something of one's own outside of oneself. Theologians are authors of their articulations and they bear significant responsibility for them, for their shape and content. Nonetheless, to the extent that these articulations are true and good, they are not simply the creations of theologians' insightful minds underpinned by their excellent lives. Theologians aren't originators of the way of life they are seeking to articulate. In terms that John's Gospel uses of Jesus himself, theologians don't come in their own name, and their teaching isn't their own (see John 5:43; 7:16).[35] In Paul's terms, theologians do not create the "treasure" but present it ever anew; instead of "proclaiming" themselves and their theologies (see 2 Cor. 4:6), theologians proclaim, each in his or her own way, Jesus Christ, who has become for them "wisdom from God, and righteousness and sanctification and redemption" (1 Cor. 1:30). At their best, theologians' visions unite with their lives in seeking to be what Paul called "the aroma of Christ," who himself is the true life (2 Cor. 2:15).

Thinking Prayer[36]

The proleptic and ecstatic character of theological life and speech is summed up in the posture and practice of prayer. Chief among the spiritual disciplines necessary to nurture the theologian's affinity with the true life, prayer is an activity of those who haven't yet arrived and who aren't sufficient in themselves. Whether

35. On the (seeming) paradox of the teaching being Christ's but not his own, see Augustine, *In Ioannis Evangelium tractatus* 29.3–5, in *Tractates on the Gospel of John 28–54*, trans. John W. Rettig, vol. 88 of *The Fathers of the Church* (Washington, DC: Catholic University of America Press, 2010), 15–17. See also Joseph Ratzinger, *Introduction to Christianity*, trans. J. R. Foster (1969; repr., San Francisco: Ignatius, 2004), 189–90.

36. We owe the title of this section to the title of Andrew Prevot's book *Thinking Prayer: Theology and Spirituality amid the Crises of Modernity* (Notre Dame, IN: University of Notre Dame Press, 2015).

it takes the form of a receptive silence before God, an insistent speech addressed to God, or the intercession of the Spirit on one's behalf (Rom. 8:26), prayer is an interior seeking for oneself and for the world to become God's home, for God's name to be hallowed, and for God's will to be done on earth as it is in heaven (Matt. 6:10). Prayer is an indispensable means of conversion, cultivating in the theologian that proleptic and ecstatic life and thought. The theologian's articulations addressed to the world issue from the theologian's own silence before and speech addressed to God and take on their character. A dimension of the way of life theologians seek to articulate, theological speech is itself always also an extended form of prayer, speaking of God and God's relation to the world always also in the first and second person and never merely the third person, as modeled by Augustine in *Confessions* and Anselm in *Proslogion*.[37]

As theologians through the centuries have known—from Dionysius the Areopagite to Teresa of Ávila, from Karl Barth and Karl Rahner to James Cone—prayer opens the eyes of the heart (Eph. 1:18).[38] Its posture of desire, adoration, and surrender disposes theologians rightly toward that of which they struggle to speak, yielding ecstatic and proleptic complexion to their articulations as the illumination of a skylight floods a whole room.[39]

37. Karl Barth, *Evangelical Theology: An Introduction*, trans. Grover Foley (New York: Holt, Rinehart and Winston, 1963), 164–65. See also Jean Leclercq and Jean-Paul Bonnes, *Un Maître de la vie spirituelle au XI siècle: Jean de Fécamp* (Paris: Librairie Philosophique J. Vrin, 1946), 76–78; Augustine, *Confessions*, trans. Henry Chadwick (Oxford: Oxford University Press, 1991), book 1, §1, p. 3.

38. Pseudo-Dionysius, *The Divine Names* 3.1, in *Pseudo-Dionysius: The Complete Works*, trans. Colm Luibheid (New York: Paulist Press, 1987), 68–69. Teresa of Ávila, *The Book of Her Life* 10.1, in *The Collected Works of St. Teresa of Avila*, trans. Kieran Kavanaugh and Otilio Rodriguez, rev. ed., vol. 1 (Washington, DC: Institute of Carmelite Studies, 1987), 105; Barth, *Evangelical Theology*, 159–70; Karl Rahner, *The Need and the Blessing of Prayer*, trans. Bruce W. Gillette (Collegeville, MN: Liturgical Press, 1997); James H. Cone, *The Spirituals and the Blues: An Interpretation* (Westport, CT: Greenwood Press, 1972).

39. The image of the skylight is Barth's. See his *Evangelical Theology*, 161. On the import of prayer for theological articulation, see, further, Prevot, *Thinking Prayer*.

Community

If prayer embodies the proleptic and ecstatic character of theologians' lives, Christian community, the extension of the Spirit-filled ministry of Christ, frames it. The Spirit who guides the work of discernment is the Mind of Christ, diffused through the church and possessed both imperfectly and communally. The theologians are not isolated units; they are members of a collective body (1 Cor. 12:27) that anticipates the eschatological unity of all in Christ (Gal. 3:28). This collective body is the theologian's bond with the people of God in every generation and spread throughout the world. The life that each theologian seeks to embody, articulate, and renew is not simply Christ's life, but Christ's life as the way of life *people of God* live in the power of the Spirit and pass on to the coming generations. Each theological articulation across times and places is rooted in that collective body and is lived in proleptic anticipation of that great eschatological throng from "every tribe, every nation, and every tongue" (Rev. 14:6).

Even that grand, ecclesial collective life points beyond itself and is both a result and an instrument of God's mission in the world, marked by unconditional love of all people—even or especially one's enemies. "The church lives from something and toward something that is greater than the church itself"—God's activity in the world aiming to make it God's home.[40] Theologians articulate visions of the true life that must grow out of and be accountable to the life of the entire people of God but that also strain toward the grand vision of the entire world becoming God's home.

Imperfect lives, imperfect articulations of the true life—yet lives that strive to align themselves with Christ's—and articulations that, rooted in this transformative striving, seek to serve Christ's mission to make the world God's home: this sort of affinity of life with the true life is what's needed for theologians to do their work well.

---

40. Miroslav Volf, *After Our Likeness: The Church as the Image of the Trinity* (Grand Rapids: Eerdmans, 1998), x.

Responsible Articulations

To do their work well, theologians must strive to align their lives with the primary Christian vision of the flourishing life. This is the main thesis of the present chapter. But throughout the entire book we have argued that the primary purpose of theology is to articulate responsibly in diverse settings the Christian vision of flourishing. The influence, then, goes both ways: from the lived lives of theologians to their theological articulations and from their theological articulations back to the lived lives of theologians—and nontheologians as well, of course. Lives and articulations illuminate and reinforce one another, to the benefit and, let's not forget, possibly to the detriment of both theology and life. Though we articulate this cycle diachronically, one element at a time, the movement of the cycle itself is synchronic and constant, and always either delivering on a promise or making good on a threat, and mostly doing a bit of both at the same time.

Language and the Shape of Life

For the influence to go both ways, articulations must be actively shaping life, rather than being, say, mere discursive echoes of lived lives themselves (lives that are themselves theological articulations to the extent that they manifest the vision of life with which they conform[41]). Articulations help not only to make a way of life plausible but also to give it direction, clarity, and depth. As evidence for the claim, consider the nature of the relation between discourse and life more generally. Language doesn't merely express experiences that are themselves prelinguistic; instead, language is partly constitutive of what we experience and how we experience it.[42] Theologians traffic in language, and the articulations they

41. Rowan Williams has persuasively reflected on this function of the lives of Christians. See Rowan Williams, *Tokens of Trust: An Introduction to Christian Belief* (Louisville: Westminster John Knox, 2007); Rowan Williams, *Teresa of Avila* (New York: Morehouse, 1991), 194–203.

42. Taylor, *Language Animal*, 4–50.

produce, dogmatic specifications included, give access to dimensions of experience that would otherwise remain inaccessible or opaque.[43] For instance, a theological account of the world as the gift of a loving God alters one's experience both of God and of the world: God is no longer a distant origin of things but an attentive Giver, and the world is not a mere thing but a gift that evokes the Giver. Similarly, theological articulations alter the nature of Christian activities in the world. For instance, relief given to sufferers in the name of Christ, possibly with the awareness that "Christ is also sick" in them,[44] is a different act with a different result than would be a seemingly identical medical intervention bereft of these convictions.

If theologians' lives shape theological articulations, which in turn shape theologians' lives, which in turn shape theological articulations . . . aren't we locked in something like a tight private dance of life and thought, a self-satisfied bubble of mutual boosting, floating above the larger reality? If so, instead of being the intelligence of the life of faith, theology would then degenerate into ideology.[45] As we see it, however, lived lives of theologians neither wholly prescribe theological articulations nor suffice to justify them epistemically.[46] Theologians are committed to a rigor-

43. Hans Urs von Balthasar has made the point compellingly with regard to mystical experiences: the careful specification of the doctrines of the faith is necessary (though not sufficient) for making the content of the Christian life legible to those who live it (see "Theology and Sanctity," 192).

44. Luther, "Fourteen Consolations," in *Luther's Works* (Philadelphia: Fortress Press, 1969), 42:122.

45. We push here, implicitly, also against Hadot, whose project very often veers in this direction, isolating the spiritual practices of ancient philosophy from the metaphysical and conceptual justifications given for them in philosophical discourse, in order to make possible their reappropriation in modernity. See Hadot, *Philosophy as a Way of Life*, 281–83.

46. There is no need here to venture far into the debates that have raged in the analytic philosophy of religion regarding the justification of religious belief. The sort of insight proffered by the alignment of one's life with the vision one seeks to articulate does not suffice on its own to justify the theological claims one may make on its basis. The affinity is necessary for gaining and articulating insights; their justification requires rigorous reasoning in which the classic sources of theological reflection (the Scriptures and the tradition of the Christian

ous search for truth and to the use of arguments that are in principle accessible to all human beings and exposed to their critique.[47] After all, we are seeking to articulate the *true* life, not just our preferred kind of life. The fact that the basic shape of this life was neither excogitated nor discovered but revealed does not diminish the obligation to truthfulness.[48] Truth seeking is a constitutive dimension of living the true life; and living the true life—always proleptically and therefore aspirationally—is a condition of the search for its truthful articulation. Michel Foucault expressed the idea well when he insisted that the act of knowledge aims to give "access to the truth" but that it can achieve this aim only if it is "*prepared, accompanied, doubled*, and *completed* by a certain transformation of the subject."[49]

The Cycle of Lives and Articulations: Theology of the Cross

Martin Luther offers a variant of the kind of cycle we advocate between the orientation of theologians' lives and reasoned critical theological articulations. We use him here to illustrate our point;

---

churches) as well as the entirety of general knowledge ought to play a role. Moreover, limiting the potential epistemic import of Christian practices to "justification" unnecessarily constrains their potentially much more capacious, if less determinate, relation to knowledge. See Robert C. Roberts and W. Jay Wood, *Intellectual Virtues: An Essay in Regulative Epistemology* (New York: Oxford University Press, 2007), 32–42. Cf. Sarah Coakley, "Dark Contemplation and Epistemic Transformation: The Analytic Theologian Re-Meets Teresa of Ávila," in *Analytic Theology: New Essays in the Philosophy of Theology*, ed. Oliver D. Crisp and Michael C. Rea (New York: Oxford University Press, 2009), 280–312.

47. On the notion of "universal criticizability," though used without reference to the affinity of lives and articulations we advocate here, see Philip Clayton, *Explanation from Physics to Theology: An Essay in Rationality and Religion* (New Haven: Yale University Press, 1989), 152.

48. For "revealed" as standing in contrast to "excogitated" and "discovered," see Friedrich Schleiermacher, *The Christian Faith* (English translation of the second German edition), ed. H. R. Mackintosh (Berkeley: Apocryphile Press, 2011), §10, pp. 49–50.

49. Michel Foucault, *Hermeneutics of the Subject: Lectures at the College du France 1981–1982*, ed. Frédéric Gross, trans. Graham Burchell (New York: Picador, 2005), 16 (emphasis ours).

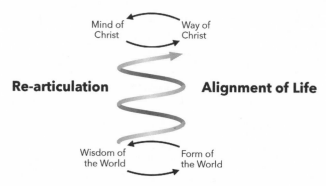

Figure 5.1 The mutual dependency between one's articulation of the vision and the direction of one's life as they ideally develop through the process of discipleship.

other variants of the cycle are possible as well. He famously, and with characteristic exaggerated sharpness, distinguished between a *theology of glory* and a *theology of the cross*, or, more frequently and more accurately, between *theologians* of glory and *theologians* of the cross.[50]

Theologians of glory produce a theology of glory when they zero in on continuity between the "perfections" of the fallen world—its virtue, justice, wisdom, glory, power, and so on—and those of God. Being oriented toward these "goods," theologians of glory perceive as false the truth of the gospel, summed up in the cross of Christ and the justification of the ungodly, and their articulations are warped accordingly: "They call the good of the cross evil and the evil of a deed good," the evil of a deed being the good deed that they falsely see as properly ascribable to the self rather than to God.[51] The taste of this "wisdom" increases their desire for it, and "they become increasingly blinded and

50. Luther, "Proceedings at Augsburg," in *Luther's Works*, 31:225; Luther, "Heidelberg Disputation," in *Luther's Works*, 31:53–55. On Luther's theology of the cross and theologians of the cross, see Forde, *Theologian of the Cross*. See also Ronald K. Rittgers, *The Reformation of Suffering: Pastoral Theology and Lay Piety in Late Medieval and Early Modern Germany* (Oxford: Oxford University Press, 2012), 111–24, and literature cited there.

51. Luther, "Heidelberg Disputation," in *Luther's Works*, 31:53.

hardened by such love," which continues to deepen the error of their theology.

Theologians of the cross, in contrast, have undergone a veritable revaluation of values at the feet of the Crucified. Their orientation toward the "manifest and visible things of God . . . , namely, his human nature, weakness, foolishness," enables them rightly to recognize God as "hidden in his suffering"[52] as the one who "loves sinners, evil persons, fools, and weaklings in order to make them righteous, good, wise, and strong."[53] Consequently, whereas a theologian of glory confuses good and evil, "a theologian of the cross calls the thing what it actually is."[54] Such theologians' orientation toward the cross warps their theology *truthfully*, which in its turn drives them back to the cross, where they recognize always anew that their very existence and all the good they have and do comes from the God whose love "flows and bestows good."[55]

As we have presented it, the contrast between theology of the cross and theology of glory seems to rest on a series of assertions. But Luther in fact first coined the phrase "theology of the cross" in the context of theological debates: in the lengthy *Explanations of Ninety-Five Theses* (1518) and in "Heidelberg Disputation" (1518). He offered *a reasoned theological argument* for the theology of the cross, aimed at persuading his detractors. More importantly, theology of the cross was central to his Reformation discovery. In a sense, his entire theological corpus—much of it consisting in detailed exposition of scriptural texts and in controversies with those he deemed theologians of glory—was a sustained argument for the vision of life toward which a theologian needs to orient her life so as to be able to do her work well. Argument was a means to help both adequate perception of the vision and reorientation of life.

What Luther observes as the key of his own vision is true of theology more generally: life and reflection whirl together in a

---

52. Luther, "Heidelberg Disputation," in *Luther's Works*, 31:52.
53. Luther, "Heidelberg Disputation," in *Luther's Works*, 31:57.
54. Luther, "Heidelberg Disputation," in *Luther's Works*, 31:53.
55. Luther, "Heidelberg Disputation," in *Luther's Works*, 31:57.

synergy either pernicious or salutary to the truth. We cannot always clearly distinguish pernicious from salutary synergies, but we can strive to obey the truth—in living our lives and in reflecting about the true life, and doing so in the community of faith. That combined striving is what makes for a good theologian.

Intellectual Dispositions

All intellectual work requires a set of dispositions, and theology especially so because it requires affinity of theological life with the vision whose articulation is theological work. Without seeking to offer an account of intellectual virtues in general, we will consider here those that are particularly important for theological work.

Love of Knowledge, God, and the World

Theology, we have argued, is a search for understanding. The *love of knowledge* is, therefore, indispensable for theological work. But what kind of knowledge? A person may be awed by the wonder of the world and gripped by the desire to understand how some aspect of it—or even the whole of it—functions; they would do well to take up a natural science. A person may be troubled by the malfunctioning of some aspect of the world and desire to figure out how to remedy the problem; they would do well to take up engineering, for instance. To be a theologian, however, a person needs to love the knowledge whose focus is the flourishing life of all creatures and whose scope encompasses the whole span of the relation between God and the world and therefore ranges from practical wisdom through the sciences to metaphysics.

Convinced that "epistemic goods are not all created equal,"[56] theologians like Augustine and Thomas Aquinas have distinguished between knowledge of a virtuous and unvirtuous sort and

56. Roberts and Wood, *Intellectual Virtues*, 156.

between genuine learning and futile curiosity.[57] To distinguish the two requires discernment. Theologians' appetite for knowledge, though very wide, must also be discriminating. They will love and seek the kind of knowledge of the relation between God and the world that is worth having.[58]

The main way to determine what kind of theological knowledge is worth having is to ask whether it is an *enactment of proper love for God and the world*—that is, whether it serves God's mission in the world. Granted, theologians will desire knowledge for its own sake; just possessing it is, arguably, an intrinsic good. But theological knowledge is also an instrumental good; its purpose is to "build up," to use Paul's term (see 2 Cor. 12:19; cf. 1 Cor. 8:1). Theologians seek knowledge as their way of participating in God's grand project of transforming the world into God's home.

Theologians themselves benefit from their knowledge, and not just by having better resources to live the true life. In the course of doing their work, theologians may acquire a measure of reputation, power, and wealth. But good theologians will not make their own cultural or monetary capital the main purpose of their work. Though they may acquire fame, they ought not to strive for it by commending themselves and their work, as did the "super apostles" of old (see 2 Cor. 10–12). Though they may wield power, they ought not to seek power (whether rhetorical, intellectual, or institutional) to enhance themselves narcissistically or to manipulate people into submission to their own way of thinking (see 1 Cor. 1:17–2:16). Though it is proper for them to receive remuneration (see 1 Cor. 9:1–18), they should not be "peddlers" whose purpose is their own enrichment (see 2 Cor. 2:17). Virtuous theologians work as God's stewards building God's home (1 Cor. 3:9), not masters building their own little empires.

57. Augustine, *Confessions* 10.35. Thomas Aquinas, *Summa Theologiae* II-II.166 and II-II.167.

58. It is not obvious, for instance, that trying to figure out how many angels can dance on the tip of a single pin is a matter of futile curiosity whereas determining how an aspect of some contemporary intellectual's thought bears on faith is genuine learning.

Love of Interlocutors

Most frequently, *love* shows up as an intellectual disposition in the phrase "hermeneutics of love." The phrase stands in contrast to "hermeneutics of suspicion," a type of interpretation Paul Ricoeur ascribed to the great "masters of suspicion" Marx, Nietzsche, and Freud: instead of seeking to restore the meaning to texts, they looked through explicit surface meanings to decode the unarticulated and hidden motivations behind the texts (class interest in the case of Marx, resentment in the case of Nietzsche, drives in the case of Freud).[59] But perhaps the alternative to a hermeneutic of suspicion is not actually a hermeneutic of *love*, as if to interpret rightly we needed to be charitable to *texts*.[60] Restoring meaning to the text does involve love, but the kind of love in view is a love for truth or the desire for knowledge—the first among the intellectual dispositions we have mentioned.

In addition to love of knowledge (the first disposition) and love of God and the world (the second disposition), there is one more love crucial to theological work: *love toward intellectual interlocutors*, especially toward opponents.[61] Theologians are scholars with a certain reputation. The centuries-old phrase *odium theologicum*—theological hatred—captures it well. One of the finest theologians of Reformation, Philip Melanchthon, considered it a benefit of death that he would be free from the harassment and anger of his fellow theologians![62] Since, as we have noted earlier, we cannot settle disagreements about God and the fundamental orientation of our lives simply by appeal to reason, theological debates easily turn into vituperative attacks and outright persecutions of those who disagree, especially when significant cultural, economic, and political goods are at stake. Love of enemies is a

59. See Paul Ricoeur, *Freud and Philosophy: An Essay on Interpretation*, trans. Denis Savage (New Haven: Yale University Press, 1970), 32–35.

60. For Ricoeur himself, the alternative to a hermeneutic of suspicion was a hermeneutic of faith. See *Freud and Philosophy*, 28–32.

61. So Roberts and Wood, *Intellectual Virtues*, 73–75.

62. George Wilson, *Philip Melanchthon: 1497–1560* (London: Religious Tract Society, 1897), 146.

central moral conviction of the Christian faith; theologians who see their work as a mode of Christian life ought to love their intellectual "enemies": to respect them as human beings, even to seek their friendship, and certainly not to let a personal squabble rob them of a good and productive argument with them.

Courage

Theologians always work within a field of social power. To a degree, all knowledge is power, and in all disciplines the search for knowledge is also a struggle for some form of power. Theology is about the home of God and therefore also about God, the object of ultimate concern, and about the true life that sets the direction of our striving. People are invested in claims about God and about true life in a way that they are not in the claims about the number of stars in a given galaxy.[63] The closer theologians come to making claims about what ought to orient human lives, the more likely they are to elicit resistance and even strong opposition. Since such claims are at the center of their work, theologians inevitably live in a socially cross-pressured space in which their reputation, their livelihood, and, in too many situations, their very lives may be at stake. In some corners of academia, simply making truth claims about the true life will be resisted. In many diverse situations, the temptation to "falsify God's word" (2 Cor. 4:2), to spin it to say what people want it to say—or what theologians *themselves* want it to say—can be strong.[64]

To be a theologian requires *courage*,[65] readiness to suffer for the claims one makes. Suffering was the lot of the prophets of the first

63. This is not to say that power is absent even from claims of the latter sort. For many years the sugar industry has, for example, manipulated what counts as knowledge about the effects of its main product. See Anahad O'Connor, "How the Sugar Industry Shifted Blame to Fat," *New York Times*, September 12, 2016, https://www.nytimes.com/2016/09/13/well/eat/how-the-sugar-industry-shifted-blame-to-fat.html.

64. Some of the most notable examples of such spin efforts, not limited to isolated theologians but part of widespread and perduring movements in the history of theology, include the denial of the freedom of religion, anti-Jewish readings of Scripture, and readings that supported the practice of slavery.

65. On the theologian's need for courage in the context of theological education situated in a market economy, see Day, "Modern Capitalism and Its Discontents."

covenant (Luke 11:47–48), the apostles of the second covenant (Acts 5:41), and Jesus Christ himself (1 Pet. 2:21). Suffering is a likely lot of all Christians: "Faith, love, *and the holy cross*" was Martin Luther's summary of the Christian life.[66] If they do their work well, theologians, too, must count on suffering and therefore need courage.

Gratitude and Humility

A boastful sense of self-importance is inappropriate for theologians. First, their main task is to point away from themselves. Karl Barth imagined the Christian theologian in the role of John the Baptist in the painting of Matthias Grünewald: he is standing to the side of the cross, holding the open Hebrew Scriptures in one hand and pointing with a finger of the other to the crucified Christ.[67] A theologian ought to draw attention to the way of life and to the one who originally embodied it, not to the intellectual prowess, fertile imagination, or dazzling rhetoric of the theologian. Inflating one's own power and wisdom detracts from the kind of power and wisdom that is an essential feature of the life theologians seek to articulate—the power that takes the form of the weakness of the crucified Christ and the wisdom that takes the form of his kind of foolishness (see 1 Cor. 1:17–25).

Second, fundamental to the way of life theologians seek to articulate and commend is the conviction that the entirety of what is, including the life and work of the theologian, is a divine gift. The proper response is *gratitude and humility*: "What do you have that you did not receive?" asked the apostle Paul rhetorically, inserting himself into a debate the Corinthians were having about his relative worth as an apostle compared to that of his impressive coworker Apollos. He continued, "And if you received it, why do you boast as if it were not a gift?" (1 Cor. 4:7). With a bit of exaggeration, he wrote to those same Corinthians, referring to

66. Martin Luther, "Sermons on the First Epistle of St. Peter," in *Luther's Works* (St. Louis: Concordia, 1967), 30:143 (emphasis ours).

67. See, for example, Karl Barth, *Church Dogmatics* I/2, ed. G. W. Bromiley and T. F. Torrance (Edinburgh: T&T Clark, 1956), 125.

himself: "I am nothing" (2 Cor. 12:11). The statement was not a self-deprecating admission of his utter worthlessness or even relative inferiority but a confident acknowledgment of the source of his competence (God's Spirit) and of the purpose of his work (pointing to Christ). That's theological humility.

Firmness—and a Soft Touch

Robert Roberts and W. Jay Wood use "firmness" to designate the nature of the "hold" we have on "epistemic goods,"[68] or, in the case of theologians, on Christian convictions and their specific articulations. Theologians' grips should not be equally firm across all epistemic goods; the claim that "the Word became flesh," for instance, should be held more firmly than the claim that "sin is a privation of the good." Still, we can state that, generally, one's grip on all theological claims should be somewhere between holding them too tightly (dogmatic rigidity) and too lightly (frivolity).

A degree of firmness is necessary for three reasons. First, it is a general feature of intellectual life that "our knowledge necessarily builds on previously formed beliefs, understandings, and experiences";[69] not holding some beliefs firmly would impair or preclude the formation of new beliefs and a deeper understanding of those we already hold.[70] Second, theologians seek to reflect on a way of life from within that way of life; without holding Christian beliefs firmly they could not continue to seek to live the Christian faith. Third, and relatedly, what theologians seek to articulate concerns the truth of human existence, the object of

68. Roberts and Wood, *Intellectual Virtues*, 184.

69. Roberts and Wood, *Intellectual Virtues*, 216.

70. It is an established position in philosophy of science that scientists ought not to give up on their hypothesis—let alone on their paradigms—too quickly. A research program can be productive even though a scientist may not be able to account for significant anomalies that the theory cannot explain. See Imre Lakatos, "Falsification and the Methodology of Scientific Research Programmes," in *Criticism and the Growth of Knowledge: Proceedings of the International Colloquium in the Philosophy of Science, London, 1965*, vol. 4, ed. Imre Lakatos and Alan Musgrave (Cambridge: Cambridge University Press, 1970), 91–196.

their ultimate love and trust, something on which they can rely in "life and death";[71] holding on to fundamental beliefs too lightly would undermine a basic trust indispensable for living.

At the same time, firmness must not degenerate into rigidity. First, rigidity would preclude honest critical examination of beliefs, an essential task of theology. Critical examination cannot even get going unless the hold on beliefs is light enough to be released. If critical examination does get going, it will need to be interrupted at some point; otherwise, the modification of individual beliefs would be impossible, let alone the rejection of the faith as a whole, which must be a possibility (if an extreme one) for the theologian's task to be a genuine matter of truth seeking. Second, and more importantly, rigidity is not fitting to the character of key Christian beliefs, such as the nature of God or of Christ. As we argued earlier, such beliefs are fundamentally *proleptic*, which is to say that one's grasp of them is always less than fully adequate and always in need of revision. Rigidity would risk generating untruthfulness. The only way to responsibly hold theological truths is with the firmness of a soft touch.

Faithfulness

As we noted earlier, theologians work on the great project of preparing the world to reach its goal of becoming God's home—and they do so knowing that Jesus Christ, God-with-us, is that home's model, architect, and builder. A home to a multitude from every language and tribe and from all periods of history, this will be theologians' home as well, so they have some personal stake in its shape, of course. But theologians aren't designing their own mansions and mapping ways to get to them. Their work is not about coming up with ideas to further their own private or collective interests. Theologians are stewards of God's home. A key qualification of a steward is faithfulness (1 Cor. 4:1–2).

71. The formulation is an echo of the first question of the Heidelberg Catechism (1563): "What is your only comfort in life and in death?"

But what does faithfulness mean when it comes to theological work? To be faithful is not simply to hold fast to what one has received, though holding fast is indispensable (1 Cor. 15:2); merely holding fast would likely amount to digging a hole in the ground and hiding the treasure, perhaps in fear of failure (see Matt. 25:18). Because the very content of what has been passed down is a *living faith*—a dynamic, adaptive way of life—to be faithful to that content is, rather, to articulate, critically examine, and commend ever anew the faith once delivered to the saints, and so to help the faith "live" in the flow of time. Theologians' faithfulness must be dynamic, not static, and improvisational, not merely replicative.

6

A Vision of Flourishing Life

If Christian theologians were to heed our call and set to work articulating a vision of flourishing life—of the *true* life—what sort of visions might emerge? We hope that we will not need to wait long to see. In this final chapter we offer our own articulation of the Christian vision of flourishing life, not a full-fledged theology of flourishing life, but a sketch of such life as we can discern and reconstruct it from the text of a single biblical writer, the apostle Paul.

In chapter 3, we proposed to use the "home of God"—or the dwelling place of God—as the overarching metaphor for developing a theology of flourishing life. The metaphor connects the first books of the Bible with the last, tying together the garden of Eden and the goal of the exodus with the "new Jerusalem," the city and the temple in one, and it shows up throughout the journey from the beginning to the end, most notably in the understanding of Christ as the dwelling place of God and in the account of both the individual follower of Christ and the entire church as the "temple of the Holy Spirit."

As we have noted earlier, other metaphors are present in Scripture as well. In the New Testament, there is no metaphor more important than the *kingdom of God*. While the metaphors of "home" and of the "kingdom" no doubt have different emphases, we argue that they are different metaphors for the same reality: flourishing life as a dynamic relation between God who is love and the world in which God dwells and which reflects God's character. The metaphor of the kingdom was central to the preaching of Jesus as recorded in the Synoptic Gospels, and even as it recedes in prevalence in other parts of the New Testament, it remains significant. The Pastoral Epistles praise God as king. Hebrews and James insist that our inheritance is a kingdom. Revelation declares the consummated reign of God. It is unusual in biblical scholarship to use the "kingdom of God" as a lens to view the main thrust of what Paul is after. This is what we propose to do here, in part because the kingdom is the tradition's earliest, even if oft-neglected, answer to the question of flourishing life.

Form and Content of the Kingdom

In Jesus's preaching, the answer to the question of flourishing life was "the kingdom of God." That's a striking response. Jesus doesn't come offering a how-to: "Six ways to a richer, more meaningful life." He doesn't merely give ethical advice. Nor does he counsel how to shield your interior life from the world around you. He proclaims and demonstrates the kingdom of God. For the Christian, then, the problem of flourishing life isn't a matter of tips and tweaks. Flourishing requires the transformative presence of the true life in the midst of the false, which requires that the true world come to be in the midst of the false world, that the world recall, recover, and for the first time fully embody its goodness as the gift of the God who is love.

As Jesus's proclamation of the kingdom indicates, the Christian answer to the question of true life has both unique *form* and unique *content*. It is not simply that Christianity offers, as do the other great world religions, a version of a "two-world" account of reality. It is not simply that there is a vision of flourishing that transcends mundane affairs and therefore norms how they ought to be conducted. Rather, the Christian faith offers a specific account of the character of the transcendent realm and how it relates to the mundane, a particular vision of God and the relation between God and the world: (1) the mundane realm has its origin in the God of love (creation); (2) having become captive to Sin, human beings live as if they and the world they inhabit were other than they truly are (sin); (3) nevertheless, the God of love has come to inhabit the mundane realm (incarnation and salvation); and (4) the mundane realm has its telos in the "new Jerusalem," the city of the one true God, the full realization of which lies in the eschatological future (consummation).[1] Taken together, these claims give the Christian account of flourishing life a complex form marked by uniquely Christian tensions between normative visions of fully flourishing life (in both protological and eschatological forms, both at creation and at the consummation) and various unfitting conditions in which our earthly lives are lived and which qualify circumstance, agency, and affect.[2] If we do not get this form right, Christian theologies of flourishing end up failing

1. We capitalize "Sin" when describing the cosmic power who, on Paul's account, tyrannizes the world; uncapitalized, "sin" denotes the human misdeeds from which this power emerges and through which this power exercises agency in the world. See Matthew Croasmun, *The Emergence of Sin: The Cosmic Tyrant in Romans* (New York: Oxford University Press, 2017), 192n1.

2. We use the word "conditions" rather than "circumstances" quite intentionally. By "conditions" we mean to indicate a set of cosmological factors or constraints that extend beyond simply the "circumstantial" aspect of life. Particularly in the apocalyptic worldview of the New Testament authors, protological, hamartiological, soteriological, and eschatological conditions shape one's agency just as much as they do one's circumstances. (Consider, for example, Ernst Käsemann's account of humankind standing under lordship in his *Commentary on Romans*, trans. G. W. Bromiley [Grand Rapids: Eerdmans, 1991], 150.) What is true of agency and circumstance is no less true of affect.

We draw attention to the "fittingness" or "unfittingness" of these conditions to indicate that it is not as though these different sets of conditions simply elicit different versions of the flourishing life. The eschatological condition—the new creation, in its fullness—is the condition most "fitting" to full flourishing and is a constitutive part of flourishing. And it is this vision that norms the others. In the present moment, this norming has an "objective" dimension to it, as (fitting) eschatological conditions are breaking into the present and drawing it forward

to be faithful either to the nature of the world as it actually is or
to the goodness of the vision of fully flourishing life.

Theology with Paul

The sketch of a vision of flourishing life that follows is more
than mere Pauline exegesis. Paul's letters are communicative in-
struments rather than theological treatises, so engaging at all with
Paul's theology entails first piecing it together from the one side
of the exchange we have access to in his letters. Doing so requires
going beyond the controversies that occasioned the letters to identify claims undergirding Paul's theology that are so fundamental
either for Paul or for both Paul and his audience that they are
assumed and therefore referenced merely obliquely and relatively
rarely.[3] These sorts of assumptions might include the content of
Paul's preaching[4] or the theological impulses that Paul and his
interlocutors would have shared. Paul's account of creation is a
good instance of this second type, shared with large swaths of his
audience: with some because they subscribed to the Jewish account
of creation and with others because they bought into something
like the Stoic common sense about creation.[5] In either case, the idea
that God created the cosmos and that this fact undergirds all our
interaction with it is clear enough for Paul and his interlocutors that
it can be argued *from* rather than argued *for* (e.g., Rom. 1:20–25).

But neither are we attempting here "Pauline theology" in the
sense of reconstructing the theology Paul worked from and articulated to his interlocutors in engaging their various questions
and controversies. Instead we offer here a self-consciously contemporary reading of Paul's theology, oriented around *our* question.

---

to eschatological consummation. But there remains a "not yet" to which New
Testament authors devote a significant amount of attention.

3. James Dunn, *The Theology of Paul the Apostle* (Grand Rapids: Eerdmans,
1998), 17.

4. For the reconstruction of the content of Paul's preaching, see, e.g., Richard B. Hays, *The Faith of Jesus Christ: The Narrative Substructure of Galatians
3:1–4:11* (Grand Rapids: Eerdmans, 2002).

5. Dunn, *Theology of Paul*, 38.

What we are doing here is not historical theology *of* Paul but rather contemporary theology *with* Paul.[6] We have our question of flourishing life, and we have it in our particular form: the tripartite question of how the true life is led well, goes well, and feels as it should. This interest will drive our engagement with Paul and will, no doubt, shape our reading of Paul—not that this matter is exogenous to Paul's theology. Just as Alain Badiou, for instance, discovered that his very modern question about universalism was actually central to Paul's thought,[7] we will find that Paul's concern is always the question of the true life in light of God's self-revelation in Jesus Christ.

We will first tackle the issue of *form* in conversation with Paul's apocalyptic framework and the way he employs it within his pastoral theology. Here, the question will be, How do the various systematic tensions entailed in any Christian vision of the good life (protological, hamartiological, soteriological, or eschatological) shape how Paul's vision of fully flourishing life in the eschaton norms the way of life he commends to his churches? Second, Paul's definition of the kingdom in Romans 14:17 will anchor our account of the *content* of the good life for Paul. We propose that Paul's tripartite definition of the kingdom ("righteousness and peace and joy in the Holy Spirit") can fruitfully be read in light of our tripartite heuristic structure of the good life (see chap. 1). Righteousness (or justice) is the substance of life led well. Peace is the substance of life going well. Joy is the substance of life feeling as it should.

— Form of the Kingdom: Advent Structure of a Life —

Much of the way Paul's apocalypticism shapes his vision of flourishing can be unpacked through sustained attention to his use of a

---

6. In this respect, we're roughly in line with the sort of approach advocated by Dale Martin in *Biblical Truths* (New Haven: Yale University Press, 2017), 5.

7. Alain Badiou, *Saint Paul: The Foundation of Universalism*, trans. Ray Brassier (Stanford, CA: Stanford University Press, 1997).

single word: *teleios*, meaning "perfect" or "mature." It is the single term that describes both the consummated reality (the "perfect" or "complete")[8] and lives lived *into* that eschatological hope and energized by its partial realization (the "mature"). That is, *teleios* can describe both ultimate and penultimate flourishing though the force of the term is different in each case. The new creation is the advent of the "complete" (*to teleion*) and as such the end of the partial (*to ek merous*) (1 Cor. 13:10[9]); lives properly oriented toward this coming reality are "mature" (again *teleios*; see 1 Cor. 2:6; 14:20; Phil. 3:15). Taken together, these two interlocking senses of the *teleios* give Paul's vision of the good life what we might call an "advent structure"; fully consummated life is entering into this world, norming this life and partly realizing itself proleptically in this life even as its full realization remains impossible under present conditions.

Two Sets of Conditions

The church is marked as that community able to discern the *teleios*—that is, able to discern the vision of fully flourishing life toward which, in the power and under the guidance of the Spirit, its members improvise life under conditions partially unfitting to it.[10] But, as is particularly clear in 1 Corinthians, one aspect of "maturity" is precisely the ability to discern the difference between these two senses of *teleios*, to avoid either an over- or underrealized eschatology.

The key is to recognize two sets of conditions—each set including a fitting and an unfitting condition—under which we live our lives. The first set is tied to the distinction between creation and consummation. Because the creation in which we live is a good

8. In this sense, *teleios* language picks up on the etymological connection to the eschatological end (*telos*) of all things (1 Cor. 10:11; 15:24).

9. The verbs here make clear that the context is eschatological transformation: the complete "comes" (*elthē*); the partial "will come to an end" (*katargēthēsetai*). *Katargeō* is here, as elsewhere, technical Pauline language of epoch change and gives *erchomai* (come) this valence in this context.

10. See, e.g., Rom. 12:2; 1 Cor. 14:20; Phil. 3:15.

gift from the God who is love (1 Cor. 10:25–26[11])—even more, the intended dwelling place of God (1 Cor. 15:28)—the present conditions under which we live our lives are fitting for true flourishing life; if we have eyes to see, literally every good thing "shimmers."[12] God created the world; therefore the mature is possible. And yet, inasmuch as that creation was from the beginning oriented toward a yet more complete consummation (15:20–49)—a final consummation that yet lies ahead of us—the present conditions are to some extent unfitting for complete flourishing life. God has not yet consummated the world, therefore the perfect, the complete, is impossible.

	Fitting	Unfitting
You and your world are . . .	Created	Not yet consummated
	Being drawn to consummation	Fallen

Table 6.1 Fitting and unfitting conditions for flourishing life, all of which obtain in the lives of all those who live in the overlap between this age and the age to come.

The second set of fitting and unfitting conditions is tied to the distinction between *fallen* creation and consummation. Because the world as we experience it is in some sense subject to Sin (e.g., Rom. 5:21; 6:6, 16–23; 7:25; 8:21) present conditions are further unfitting for true flourishing life. Because of sin, the perfect is impossible. Yet, inasmuch as we are those on whom the ends of the ages have come (1 Cor. 10:11) in the in-breaking *adventus* of God in the life of Christ, which is the inaugurated coming

11. "Eat whatever is sold in the meat market without raising any question on the ground of conscience, for 'the earth and its fullness are the Lord's.'" As is often the case, Paul argues *from* rather than *for* his doctrine of creation, citing Psalm 24:1 as support for enjoying the good things of creation (in this case, the meat in the marketplace) as gifts from God.

12. Miroslav Volf, *Flourishing: Why We Need Religion in a Globalized World* (New Haven: Yale University Press, 2015), 204–5.

of the kingdom of God, present conditions are fitting for true flourishing life. Because of Christ entering the world, the mature is possible.

The *teleios* both (1) stands in opposition to Sin and (2) describes the telos of creation in consummated relation to God. In the sin-redemption subplot, *teleios* describes that which has been set free from the dominion of Sin and has the possibility of doing the good (*teleios* as "mature"; e.g., 1 Cor. 2:6). In the primary creation-consummation plot, *teleios* describes that which has been and/or is being drawn to consummation (*teleios* as "perfect" or "complete"; e.g., 1 Cor. 13:10).

In Paul's letters, the two sets of unfitting conditions are usually conflated. Rather than distinguishing between all four of these tensive poles, Paul's language instead tracks the disjunction between "this age" and "the age to come." In this schema, both sorts of unfitting conditions are characteristic of "this age." As a result, both the nature of created-but-not-yet-consummated bodies and the reality of sin can be captured in a single multivalent word, *sarx* ("flesh"). *Sarx* describes the sorts of bodies that exist in this age, bodies that cannot by their nature inherit the kingdom of God because they are corruptible.[13] There is a tragic character to life "in the flesh," even, in theory, apart from sin.[14] As a result of *both* their structural corruptibility *and* the contingent fact of sin, in this age, fleshly bodies are universally subject to the rule of Sin and are themselves members of the body of Sin.[15] So *sarkikos* for Paul can

13. On the impossibility of flesh inheriting the kingdom, see 1 Cor. 15:50. Dunn argues that "weak and corruptible" captures the heart of Pauline ambivalence about *sarx* (*Theology of Paul*, 70). We would note that these two categories also nearly capture the possible content of just the not-yet-consummated set of unfitting conditions, as distinguished from the conditions that follow from the dominion of Sin.

14. The comparison of the body to a "clay jar" in 2 Cor. 4:7 speaks to the fragility of earthly life.

15. On membership in the collective body of Sin, see Rom. 6:6 and Matthew Croasmun, *The Emergence of Sin: The Cosmic Tyrant in Romans* (New York: Oxford University Press, 2017), 111–25. The universal dominion of Sin over flesh is the reason why, as Paul invites his churches to embrace the mature mode of flourishing that is free from Sin's dominion, he has to insist, in a certain sense

capture both sets of "unfitting" conditions, the conditions under which we must improvise the true life in the power of the Spirit. It is for this reason that *sarkikos* (and its corresponding psychological term, *psychikos*) is so often pitted against *pneumatikos* ("spiritual") in Paul's writing.[16] In the overlap of the ages, the "spiritual" life is the true and ultimately enduring eschatological life breaking into the false and fading "fleshly" life.

A Partly Realized Eschatology

Because of these conditions, the flourishing life is lived *into* a life that can never be fully realized this side of the eschaton. Indeed, the argument of 1 Corinthians is largely an argument about how these two senses of *teleios* relate: What does being mature in this life have to do with the perfect or complete that comes at the final consummation? An overrealized eschatology attempts to achieve the perfect in ways that are rendered incoherent by the conditions of this life (i.e., [1] sin, inasmuch as its dominion constrains our willing and knowing and, therefore, our agential flourishing, and [2] the corruptible nature of created bodies). Recognition of the "unfittingness" of *some* of the conditions under which we live our lives is a necessary component of true Pauline maturity. The life we lead in the time between the times is to be imaginatively improvised *into* the consummated life,[17] or, better yet, through participation in a modality of eschatological life that is entering this world and drawing us forward toward its completion.

---

counterfactually, that they are "not in the flesh" (8:9); for similar reasons, Paul holds that the complete life of the consummated kingdom cannot be inherited by "flesh and blood" (1 Cor. 15:50). To the extent to which they are in the flesh, they are subject to Sin. Freedom from Sin requires freedom from the flesh, which can only be realized through the sort of "as if not" posture we describe below.

16. See especially 1 Cor. 15:45–46, which demonstrates that, for Paul, *psychē* ("soul") describes the creation in this age—that is, apart from consummation (the nature of the pristine-but-unconsummated Adam, following Gen. 2:7)—while *pneuma* ("spirit") characterizes life in the age to come (Christ, the last Adam, the life-giving spirit).

17. For Paul's discussion of what we are calling imaginative improvisation *into* the consummated flourishing life, see 1 Cor. 7:29–31; 9:19–23.

We see this in Pauline preaching, for example, in the ways that the Pauline baptismal slogan of Galatians 3:28 was received in Corinth and in Paul's response to this reception. Galatians 3:28 paints a vivid picture of consummated flourishing life "in Christ Jesus": "There is no longer Jew nor Greek, no longer slave nor free, no longer 'male and female.'"[18] On its face, and in line with much apocalyptic fervor, this slogan announces a set of present-tense realities. And so it is understandable that, in a Corinthian church in which, despite his protestations, Paul had practiced baptism,[19] confusion abounds around questions of cultural categories, class distinction, and sexual difference.[20] The confusions arise because no matter how much the church members live into the unity they have "in Christ Jesus," no matter how committed they are to the equality of Jew and Greek, the equality of slave and free, or even the eschatological dissolution of sexual difference, "this world" remains. Cultural markers retain their status, class differences are social realities regardless of liberative patterns of ecclesial life, and bodies remain sexed, gendered, and valued according to patriarchal frameworks. "This world" can be transformed—indeed, through the work of baptism, the new creation is coming to be in the midst of the old[21]—but only within the parameters set by its not-yet-consummated character.

Paul names clearly the error of the "strong" in the Corinthian community in 1 Corinthians 4:8: "Already you are full! Already you have become rich! Apart from us, you reign![22] Indeed I wish

18. Authors' translation.

19. In 1 Cor. 1:14–16, Paul concedes that he has baptized a number of folks in the Corinthian church.

20. For confusion about cultural categories, see 1 Cor. 8:1–8; for confusion about class distinctions, see 1 Cor. 1–2; for confusion about sexual difference, see 5:1.

21. "So if anyone is in Christ, there is a new creation: everything old has passed away; see, everything has become new!" (2 Cor. 5:17).

22. The aorist tense of the verb—which we have translated in the present tense as "reign" in order to draw out the connection to Rom. 5:17—further emphasizes that the problem lies in the "strong" having misidentified their place "temporally" in the narrative structure of God's relating with the world. They believe they "became kings" already; rather, it is the case that they *will reign in life* (Rom. 5:17, authors' translation).

that you would reign, in order that we also could reign with you" (authors' translation). We will take up the *content* of Paul's complaints later as we talk about the content of Paul's vision of flourishing, but the *form* of his critique is clear: the problem is an overrealized "already." They will indeed reign one day,[23] but *not yet*. To consider oneself to have fully realized this aspect of the *teleios* ("perfect") vision of flourishing life constitutes a failure to have lived that vision under the present conditions; this failure is an ironic sign that the "strong" Corinthians are not yet *teleios* ("mature"). An overrealized eschatology both misconstrues the conditions under which we live and is arrogant about how much of the true life—even the true life that *is* possible under the conditions of the false—we have realized in our own lives.

However, overrealization isn't Paul's only concern when it comes to his churches' eschatology. Underrealization is at least as great a threat and is often the ironic result of the arrogant blindness to our own lives that an overrealized eschatology cultivates. And underrealization, too, threatens the Corinthian church. The wisdom and power structures of this world still hold sway within the church itself, so arguments about status abound (1 Cor. 3; 4:8–10). Corinthian Christians still take one another to court, failing to live oriented toward a future in which "the saints will judge the world" (6:1–2). Most troubling of all, for Paul, is the Corinthians' grossly underrealized unity in Christ, the crown of the Galatian baptismal slogan: "All of you are one in Christ Jesus" (Gal. 3:28). Were we to adopt a vision of flourishing life with an underrealized eschatology, we might, by lowering the bar on how much of the fully consummated vision of flourishing we can hope to achieve this side of the eschaton, inappropriately excuse these sorts of failings.

Spirit-Led Improvisation

What then should we do? Paul is willing neither to capitulate to the overrealized eschatology nor to surrender the vision

---

23. The promise of their reign in the consummated kingdom is in Rom. 5:17.

of eschatological flourishing toward which he has oriented his churches. His response is to invite the Corinthians to a practice of imaginative improvisation—Spirit-led, discerning, and wise—living in an "as if not" posture toward these unfitting conditions and their consequences. "From now on, let even those who have wives be as though they had none, and those who mourn as though they were not mourning, and those who rejoice as though they were not rejoicing, and those who buy as though they had no possessions, and those who deal with the world as though they had no dealings with it" (1 Cor. 7:29–31). The explanation has an eschatological basis: "For the present form [*schēma*] of this world is passing away" (7:31).[24] Living "as if not" means taking into account the reality of living at the overlap of the ages. In light of the soon-no-longer-but-nevertheless-still presence of these unfitting conditions ("the form of this world") and the opposition they present,[25] the Corinthians have to improvise lives in the context of considerable tension. The vision of fully consummated flourishing life (e.g., as expressed in Gal. 3:28) lays demands on this improvisation (indeed, the consummated vision is the telos of reality), but the unfitting conditions of the world and the ways they persistently menace flourishing life must also be attended to. Paul models this improvisation as he performs various identities radically relativized by the Galatian baptismal formula's declaration that "there is no longer Jew nor Greek, no longer slave nor free" (Gal. 3:28, authors' translation). Living *toward* a world in which these identities no longer divide, but living *in* a world fundamentally structured by them, Paul takes up and lays down various identities for the sake of the gospel. Though free, he has made himself a slave. For the sake of the gospel, he lives sometimes as one under the

24. The passing away of this "form" (*schēma*) is also in view in Rom. 12:2, in which not being conformed (*syschēmatizesthe*) to this world and instead being transformed (*metamorphousthe*) is the prerequisite for being able to discern what is good and acceptable and perfect (*teleion*).

25. For the opposition presented by the unfitting conditions of the present age, see, e.g., 1 Cor. 2:6–8.

Jewish law, other times as one free from it—all while recognizing the truth of his situation as one no longer under "the law" but nevertheless under "Christ's law." Paul becomes "all things to all people" in the flow of a wise, Spirit-led improvisation (1 Cor. 9:19–23).

This improvisation is not free in a Nietzschean sense,[26] but rather strives for a goal: consummated flourishing life. Even if this goal is something that cannot be fully articulated, life in the here and now can be true life in striving for this goal in Christ, by the Spirit.[27] The typical Pauline image is that of running a race.[28] Living honestly in light of eschatological tension means recognizing that reaching this goal is impossible in this life—"not that I have already obtained this or have already reached the goal"—but it is one we aim at, even strive for, through imaginative improvisation in the power of the Spirit: "But I press on to

26. Friedrich Nietzsche, *The Gay Science: With a Prelude in Rhymes and an Appendix of Songs*, trans. Walter Kaufmann (New York: Random House, 1974), §124, p. 180: "We have left the land and have embarked. We have burned our bridges behind us. . . . Beside you is the ocean. . . . You will realize that it is infinite and that there is nothing more awesome than infinity."

27. On the impossibility of fully describing consummated flourishing life, see, e.g., 1 Cor. 2:9. Nevertheless, the centrality of this telos distinguishes our reading of Paul's language from Giorgio Agamben's treatment of "as not" in *The Time That Remains: A Commentary on the Letter to the Romans*, trans. Patricia Daily (Stanford, CA: Stanford University Press, 2005), 19–43. The distinction between our reading and Agamben's will by now be familiar: Agamben's reading works hard to avoid articulating positive content, finding in the "as not" only an opportunity for freedom from various constraints. Agamben's reading renders Paul as advocating negation only, whereas we argue that Paul's negation is in service of an affirmation of an in-breaking flourishing life that flies many banners in the Pauline text: edification (Rom. 14:19), evangelization (1 Cor. 9:23), and unity (Gal. 3:28). This life is the goal of Pauline "use" of various this-worldly goods.

Agamben also gets the grammar of 1 Cor. 7:29–31 wrong, essentially reading *hōs mē* as *hōs ou*, and therefore misconstrues the substance of Paul's point. The implied counterfactual condition embedded in the use of *mē* reminds the reader of the enduring reality of the present form of the world—even as it is passing away. The Christian imaginatively improvises her life *as if* the world were other than it is—even though it in fact persists.

28. See 1 Cor. 9:24; Gal. 2:2; 5:7; Phil. 2:16.

make it my own, because Christ Jesus has made me his own" (Phil. 3:12).

Created Goodness and Inaugurated Eschatology

The dawning of the age to come isn't the only reason we have the possibility of experiencing—and the responsibility to realize—something of the fullness of flourishing life. Created goodness, though known to us only as *sarx*—that is, in the fragility of its protological state and always refracted through the corruption of sin—nevertheless continues to ground the possibility of flourishing life.[29] God is not just the one "to whom" the world is oriented in its eschatological consummation but also the one from whom and through whom it has come into being (Rom. 11:36). For this reason, Paul is convinced that "nothing is unclean in itself" (Rom. 14:14), and, along with the psalmist, he can affirm that "the earth and its fullness are the Lord's" (1 Cor. 10:26). Many appearances of the good life in *this* life—the sweetness of a strawberry or the giggle of a newborn—are simply results of this divine goodness mediated to us in the creation. As Paul insists, God's power and nature are manifest in the creation, and the proper human response is honor and gratitude.[30] All food and drink, whether explicitly taken up into the symbolic world of the kingdom through Eucharist or not, and every activity undertaken within God's creation are opportunities for the unveiling of the glory of God.[31] The world that longs to be set free is not merely *kosmos* but *ktisis*—not merely world but creation.[32] It is created goodness and inaugurated eschatological fulfillment *together* that give form to the true life and lay on us the responsibility to live it.

29. James Dunn argues persuasively that Paul's relative silence regarding creation is not because the foundational goodness of creation is unimportant to Paul, but rather because "God's role as creator is [a] fundamental taken-for-granted of Paul's theology." Dunn, *Theology of Paul*, 38.
30. On the creation as the manifestation of God's nature and power, see Rom. 1:20. On gratitude as the proper human response, see Rom. 1:21; 1 Thess. 5:18.
31. "So, whether you eat or drink, or whatever you do, do everything for the glory of God" (1 Cor. 10:31).
32. Rom. 8:19–23.

Placed in this set of tensions (protological, hamartiological, soteriological, and eschatological), in the power of the Spirit and following Christ, we live into the fully flourishing life that calls us forward. In so doing, we must construe the world rightly. First, we must construe the world as created good by God, meaning that material goods are not merely things but relations, gifts from the God of love, given equally to all. Second, we ought to see the world as malformed by sin, recognizing how the world is broken, especially how ungodly power has distorted the world and enthroned its distortions as "natural," apparently usurping the rightful priority of creation. Third, we ought to construe the world as the site of God's indwelling in the person of Jesus Christ, seeing the redemption of all things currently and incompletely underway. Finally, we must construe the world as destined for eschatological consummation, seeing the world both in hope and with sober awareness that the world is not yet what it will one day be.

Awareness of these tensions makes it possible to willingly accept certain limitations to flourishing without giving up on the vision of its fullness. Take, for example, poverty as a cost of discipleship. We can embrace it without idealizing it or turning our attention away from the poverty of others—or, worse yet, losing the ability to recognize lack of sufficient resources to flourish as less than God's best for people. This awareness points the way to embrace suffering without idealizing it to the extent that we can no longer work to relieve the suffering of others. It points the way to mourning with those who mourn without perversely making mourning our good. It allows us to mourn while lamenting the fact that we must mourn, longing for joy, even in some sense "rejoicing always." Awareness of these tensions, in short, allows us neither to let the cost of engagement with the world's brokenness deter us from engaging fully nor to let the cost confuse us about the nature of the good for the sake of which we accepted that cost in the first place—or of the goodness of the God who invites us, *calls* us to flourishing life.

––––––––––– **Content of the Kingdom** –––––––––––

We have examined thus far the *form* of the Christian vision of flourishing, the set of tensions in which it exists. But what is the *content* of the kingdom—what is the character of life coming to be within these tensions? The apostle Paul describes the content of the kingdom in Romans 14:17: "For the kingdom of God is not food and drink but righteousness and peace and joy in the Holy Spirit." While this verse appears in the midst of a communal dispute about dietary restrictions for members of the church, the diction and content of the definition are independent of the polemical context; they are a compact summary of a Christian vision of true life that Paul can import in order to adjudicate the question at hand.[33]

We propose that this set of three, "righteousness and peace and joy"—and each "in the Holy Spirit"—offers answers to the three questions with which we began the chapter. What does it mean for life to be led well? It is righteous. What does it mean for life to go well? It is peaceful. And what does it mean for life to feel as it should? It is full of joy. Here we approach each as we approach Paul's texts more broadly: not primarily excavating historical meaning but thinking theologically with Paul in our setting and with our questions. What does the flourishing life look like in each of its three aspects? How are these three related? And how does the advent structure of the Christian vision of flourishing refract each of these as we strive to realize them in the here and now?

Life Led Well

First of all, we have *dikaiosynē*, which we will render variously as "righteousness" or "justice."[34] It is an understatement to say

33. Aquinas read this passage as offering precisely such a definition—and as set within the sorts of tensions Paul's apocalypticism identifies. In defining the kingdom, says Aquinas, Paul articulates the substance of the good of the human being: "Three things . . . possessed imperfectly in this life, but perfectly when the saints will possess the kingdom God prepared for them" (*In ad Rom*. C.14 L.2, 1128).

34. In contemporary English, "righteousness" tends to *denote* almost nothing—nobody outside Christian theology would ever use the word—and *connote* "self-

that the meaning of *dikaiosynē* has been contested in the history of the interpretation of Paul.[35] But this needn't prevent us from seeing something rather straightforward: in Paul, *dikaiosynē* is about *covenant faithfulness*. Primarily, especially in Romans, it refers to God's covenant faithfulness in God's righteous rule over creation.[36] But the *dikaios* root can also refer to Jesus, who, crucially, performed the just act (the *dikaiōma*) we could not.[37] This is the act of obedience that accomplishes what the law could not, bringing about not merely a forensic fiction but the actual possibility that "the just requirement of the law might be fulfilled in us, who walk not according to the flesh but according to the Spirit" (Rom. 8:4). That is, when Paul talks about *dikaiosynē* with respect to us, he refers, of course, not only to our *lack* of

righteousness," the opposite of what Paul might have meant by *dikaiosynē*. On the plus side, this means that we can use the word "righteousness" to mean more or less whatever we'd like it to mean. And it has the advantage of being cognate with the word "right," which can be helpful. "Justice," in contemporary English, tends to accurately denote a small subset of what Paul might have meant by *dikaiosynē*. We can't help but think about "justice" in terms of *equity* and restrict ourselves to this sense (even Aquinas seems to get sidetracked by this: see *Summa Theologiae* II-II.58.11). In some circles, the word "justice" adds to this restricted sense of *dikaiosynē* something that Paul would never have intended, namely, *retribution*. When we use "justice" to translate *dikaiosynē*, we will need to resist these tendencies.

35. For biblical scholars of a previous generation, *dikaiosynē* was a term that meant one thing for Paul—namely, the forensic status of the recipient of God's "sovereign and gracious and decisive intervention for man in Christ" (*Theological Dictionary of the New Testament*, vol. 2, ed. Gerhard Kittel, trans. G. W. Bromiley [Grand Rapids: Eerdmans, 1964], 203)—and quite another in the rest of the New Testament—namely, "the right conduct of man which follows the will of God and is pleasing to Him, for rectitude of life before God" (Kittel, *Theological Dictionary*, 2:198). While we don't have space to make the argument here, suffice to say that the New Perspective on Paul has rescued us from this confusion. As E. P. Sanders explains: "As the essence of salvation, righteousness is not forensic . . . since salvation itself is not conceived of forensically as acquittal, but as life in Christ Jesus." "Patterns of Religion in Paul and Rabbinic Judaism: A Holistic Method of Comparison," *Harvard Theological Review* 66, no. 4 (October 1973): 470n46.

36. See, e.g., Rom. 1:17; 3:5, 21–26.

37. The *dikaiōma* is the "just act" of Christ that leads to justification and life for all in Rom. 5:18.

righteousness, but also to the ideal of a righteous or just way of life.[38]

So, righteousness is fidelity to the covenant[39]—and, when all is right, there is an alignment of the faithfulness of God to God's people and of God's people to God, through their participation in Christ's faithfulness. But this is still rather formal. *Of course* justice is fidelity to the covenant through obedience to the law. But what is the content of the covenant? What is the substance of the law to which we ought to be obedient? In Paul, the answer is crystal clear: the content of the covenant is obedience to the law of love.[40] There is a parallel, then, between the triad of Romans 14:17 (justice, peace, and joy) and the beginning of the description of the fruit of the Spirit in Galatians 5:22: *love, joy,* and *peace* (Gal. 5:22). Given the centrality of love as that which sums up the law for Paul, that which specifies the content of justice in a modality of benevolent self-giving, we could just as easily—and perhaps with more precision—define the kingdom as "*love* and peace and joy in the Holy Spirit." A flourishing agency marks the flourishing life as a life of *love.* This is what it means to lead one's life well, to be *righteous* or *just in the Spirit* in the kingdom of God.

Love is not just the material description of the Christian account of life led well. It also has primacy among the three aspects of flourishing life as that life is realized under the present unfitting conditions, for what we can say about love as being no less *love* for its existing under unfitting conditions, we cannot say about peace and joy. Under unfitting conditions, we will have circumstances that cannot truthfully be described as *peaceful.* Under unfitting conditions, the truthful emotional response cannot and will not

38. So, Käsemann goes too far when he says that "righteousness is not right action . . . but divine power" (*Commentary on Romans,* 377). It is both.

39. This formulation is applicable to both human righteousness and God's. According to Dunn, "It should equally be evident why God's righteousness could be understood as God's *faithfulness* to his people. For his righteousness was simply the fulfillment of his covenant obligation as Israel's God in delivering, saving, and vindicating Israel, despite Israel's own failure." *Theology of Paul,* 342.

40. Rom. 13:10; Gal. 5:14.

always be *joy*. But even under unfitting conditions, we, in principle though not in actuality, can always act in love. Love can be fully expressed and realized in the here and now—even if it often has a peculiar shape. That is, the Christian ought to say "always and only love." We ought *not* to say "always and only rejoice." The Christian ought *always* to rejoice—and so Paul commands in Philippians 4:4—but even while rejoicing always, we must, in Paul's vision of the good life, mourn with those who mourn (Rom. 12:15). The Christian ought not to expect always and only to be at peace. We can say "always and only *make* peace," but only because that's what love does when peace is lacking. Love will always have primacy in the realization of flourishing life under the unfitting conditions of the present age.

This life of love is at the very heart of the creation. As much as Paul is happy to describe the saints as "those who love God" (Rom. 8:28), even more decisive is the image of an active divine love, revealed most potently in the life, death, and resurrection of Christ, but nevertheless suffused throughout the creation (8:39). The law of love of neighbor, then, is "holy" (7:12) in part because it corresponds to the nature of a world created good by the holy God who is love in God's very being and whose every act is therefore an expression of love. The fullness of our lives, however, lies decidedly ahead of us in the consummated kingdom.

The fully consummated life, too, is a life of love. As Paul is at great pains to insist in 1 Corinthians 13, love is what is held in common between this age and the age to come; it is that which remains eschatologically. Along with the bodily continuity Paul describes in 1 Corinthians 15:35–57, the continuity of love reveals that the world to come is not some other world, but rather this world transformed. Love underwrites the transition from this age to the next, from the creation's immaturity to its mature consummation as the home of God. In this fullness, in the perfection of its active dimension, flourishing human life is a universal exercise of love generously given and gratefully received, a participation in the consummated divine reign spoken of in Romans 5:17, which operates in life-giving love. The reign of love is a shared reign (*basileusousin* in Rom. 5:17 is plural), the very height of true collaboration and the interweaving of interdependent agencies, marked by unity of mind and thought.[41] This efficacious and noncompetitive reign of love both (1) heals the impotence that Sin has wrought in human agency[42] and (2) overcomes the fundamentally competitive nature of agency in created-but-not-yet-consummated finitude. The fully consummated life of love brings about the good that it wills, and that good is beneficial not just for part of the creation but for the creation as a whole. In the fully realized kingdom, life led well is the flourishing of a love that reigns together.

And yet, the life we will live in the consummated kingdom is not possible here and now. Rather, the true life to which we are called—flourishing life under the present conditions of sin and corruptibility—is a life of love, but this is often a love that suffers. To be clear, not all love in the proleptic flourishing life will be love that suffers. The fitting conditions of creation will mean that some acts of love will find even this world genial to love's expression and ensue in love's joyful reception. And not all suffering in this world is the consequence of love. Much suffering in this life is due to sin—our own and the sin of others—and much of it follows from our fragility and temporality. As a life coming to be in the midst of a world that is, in part, unfitting to it, the proleptic flourishing life is often marked by a love that suffers. If consummated flourishing agency is marked by perfect reciprocity, cooperation, and unity of purpose, penultimate flourishing agency aims at this cooperation and unity in service of love,[43] and yet lives aware that love will elicit opposition under the unfitting conditions of this life. Paradigmatically, this opposition comes from "the rulers of this age" who "crucified the Lord of glory" (1 Cor. 2:8). To these rulers—and the dominant structures that are coming to nothing in Christ but are not yet nothing—the true life will appear false. The very power of God—the logos

41. For this unity, see, e.g., 1 Cor. 1:10; Phil. 2:2.
42. The climax of the agential impotence brought about by sin is Rom. 7:18: "I can will what is right, but I cannot do it."
43. See, e.g., Rom. 14:19; 1 Cor. 8:1; 2 Cor. 12:19.

of the cross—will look like foolishness (1:18). And yet the cross was the efficacious act of self-giving love par excellence. It appeared ineffective—but only to those without eyes to see. Similarly, those who would follow in Jesus's footsteps ought to expect their "reign" in this life to look like the comically ineffective but cosmically efficacious "reign" of Christ on the cross. Their love will often be a love that suffers.

Our attempts to walk according to the law of love are opposed not only by "the rulers of this age" but also by our very selves. Sin corrupts and weakens our agency, both causing us to sin and preventing us from doing the good—or, in the most extreme cases, frustrating our agency as such (Rom. 7:15). The predicament Paul describes in Romans 7 is not foreign to the Christian who is trying to live the life of love; we know ourselves always as *simul justus et peccator*.[44] As a result, the proleptic life of love always strives for justice and yet also lives with the awareness of one's status nevertheless as sinner. This means that proleptic flourishing life will be marked by a suspicion of "power"—first of all, one's own. Living *into* the life of love as a sinner means living always aware that we "have not yet laid hold of" the life toward which we are striving—we have not yet been "perfected"—but, rather, we look in every circumstance to "be laid hold of" (Phil. 3:12[45]) by the one whose love we seek to have live through us.

Even this resistance—internal and external—only further cements the primacy of love in the proleptic flourishing life. While the *fact* of love—its goodness and centrality—reveals the *continuity* of

44. Here we follow James Dunn in reading Rom. 7 as describing the life of the believer living at the overlap of the ages (*Romans 1–8*, Word Biblical Commentary 38A [Grand Rapids: Zondervan, 1988], 377). What Paul describes is a universal human condition. For us, Stanley Stowers's comparisons of the various tellings of the Medea story in the ancient world prove not that the addressees of the letter were universally gentile but rather that the situation Paul describes would have been understood—by all ancient listeners—as a universal human plight. Stanley Stowers, *A Rereading of Romans: Justice, Jews, and Gentiles* (New Haven: Yale University Press, 1994), 270–72. For *simul justus et peccator*, see Martin Luther, *Lectures on Galatians*, in *Luther's Works* (St. Louis: Concordia, 1963), 26:232.

45. Authors' translation.

the eschatological transition, the *shape* of love reveals the *discontinuity*. Love in the consummated kingdom reigns; love betwixt and between often suffers. This is why the message of the cross is foolishness to this world (1 Cor. 1:18). The irreconcilable differences between this age and the age to come have consequences not only for the shape of love but also for its misrecognition. As a result, the way of love in the overlap of the ages means embracing the so-called weakness and foolishness of the cross, which are in fact the very strength and wisdom of God.[46]

Life Going Well

If the righteousness of love is Paul's answer to the question of how to characterize a life led well, when asked what circumstances make for flourishing life, his answer is peace. While it is clear that "peace" in Paul's writing can describe something of an inner disposition,[47] it is equally clear that, on the whole, the term has a more objective quality; *eirēnē* describes a state of the world, a world set right.[48] In Romans 14:17, the close context suggests that

46. Paul's wise, Spirit-led improvisation of sociocultural identity is subject to this misrecognition, as we learn in 2 Corinthians. The one who became "all things to all people" (1 Cor. 9:22) has earned the reputation of an imposter and one who is unknown (2 Cor. 6:8–9); the one who "became weak" (1 Cor. 9:22) is now seen as dying, punished, sorrowful, poor, and having nothing (2 Cor. 6:9–10). All of this exists in stark contrast to the reality visible to those who discern spiritually: that Paul and his compatriots are in fact true, well known, alive, not killed, rejoicing, rich, and possessing everything (2 Cor. 6:8–10).

47. E.g., Rom. 15:13, where it appears alongside *joy*.

48. On the objective quality of *peace*, Stanley Porter's definition is typical in "Peace, Reconciliation," in *Dictionary of Paul and His Letters*, ed. Gerald F. Hawthorne and Ralph P. Martin (Downers Grove, IL: IVP Academic, 1993), 695. The cosmic scope of Paul's concern is most prominent in 1 Cor. 15 and Rom. 8. Assuming that Paul's concept of *eirēnē* is conditioned by the Hebrew concept of *shalom* (which would have been an influential idea for Paul), a quite expansive set of circumstances might well be in view in many cases of Paul's use of the term, particularly in a definition like we have in Rom. 14:17. So James Dunn: "Peace here [in Paul] is not to be restricted to the Greek idea of the cessation of war, or to be merely spiritualized (inner calm). It will certainly include the much richer Hebrew concept of *shalom*, where the basic idea is of 'well-being,' including social harmony and communal well-doing." Dunn, *Theology of Paul*, 387.

the meaning of "peace" here is precisely about flourishing circumstances—particularly right relationships.[49] Indeed, at the heart of Paul's vision of life going well is a set of peaceful relationships—with God and, on the foundation of relationship with God, with other people and the created world.[50]

None of these relationships is unmarked by sin: "All, both Jews and Greeks, are under the power of Sin," with the result that "the way of peace they have not known" (Rom. 3:9, 17). But God's gracious work of justification—the invitation to participation in the divine way of justice—makes possible a new, restored "peace with God" (5:1). This right relationship with God provides the foundation of flourishing life, both at the consummation of all things and along the way.

Taking the eschatological perspective first, in Paul's apocalyptic framework, the consummated kingdom is *a whole world at peace with God*; this is the fulfillment of what it means for life to go well. The fundamental eschatological circumstance is the reign of God, not as some aloof cosmic despot, but rather as an intimate

---

It might be objected that Paul's professed ability to be content with whatever he has (Phil. 4:12) means that, for Paul, circumstances are irrelevant to the flourishing life. And, indeed, a stridently Stoic reading of Paul would come to precisely this conclusion. At least two significant factors militate against this reading of Paul. First, Paul affirms the goodness of creation and everything in it (1 Cor. 10:26) and frequently demonstrates concern for the distribution of material goods (as discussed below) in ways that suggest that material circumstances are important. Second, and perhaps more significantly, Paul expects an eschatological transformation of life's circumstances, including the liberation of the material world. Along with the gift of the Son, we can expect God to give us "all things." Paul's advocacy of self-mastery (*autarkeia*) is not a Stoic denigration of material circumstances, but rather a strategy for life at the overlap of the ages. In a world where the righteous way of love engenders opposition, bad circumstances—while genuinely regrettable—are inevitable and, at times, even signs of one's obedience to the way of love and, therefore, causes for joy. It is only in light of these peculiar conditions that self-mastery becomes desirable.

49. Romans 12:18 calls on the hearers to "live peaceably with all [*meta pantōn anthrōpōn eirēneuontes*]," foregrounding a relational state of affairs. Romans 14:19, two verses after our definition, similarly uses the word "peace" to denote a desirable state of affairs: "Let us then pursue what makes for peace [*eirēnēs*]."

50. For relationship with God see, e.g., Rom. 5:1; with other people, 14:19; with the creation, 8:22.

Father.[51] God's eschatological reign is a reign of presence. In the end, when the kingdom of God comes in its fullness, God is "all in all" (1 Cor. 15:28): the creation is suffused with the divine presence, and the world becomes the home of God.

The restored peace in the relationship with God rectifies other relationships; in the fully flourishing life, peace with God brings *peace with others and with the creation as a whole*. Peace in human affairs begins in the church. The ultimate consummated vision—to be realized as appropriate in the time between the times—is of a startling unity in Christ that spans divides of ethnicity, class, and sex (Gal. 3:28). Paul has various images for this unity—chiefly, the body of Christ and the adopted family of God—but, taken together, they emphasize a unity in diversity and an intimacy with one another and with God.[52] What begins with the family of God extends to the entire creation, whose consummated future is tied to that of the children of God (Rom. 8:18–25). If the fallen world projects an illusion of human independence from the creation, the cosmic scope of Paul's vision of eschatological transformation insists that fully flourishing human life is inseparable from the flourishing of the creation as a whole. In the end, all creation is embraced by the peace that was birthed in the church.

In the proleptic flourishing life, as we have right *relationship with God*, the peace of the kingdom breaks in, transforming circumstances. And so the experience of peace—never complete and never unassailable by the enemies of God (often, ourselves)—is nevertheless possible in proleptic broken communal enactments. In the coming of the kingdom we can have a foretaste of the peace of the kingdom, chiefly in the presence of God's Spirit, a down payment on the intimacy with God that is the foundation of the consummated kingdom.[53] This divine presence can transform our

51. For the reign of God, see, e.g., 1 Cor. 15:24–28; for the intimacy of God's relation as Father, see Rom. 8:15.

52. For the "body of Christ," see Rom. 12 and 1 Cor. 12. For the family of God, see Rom. 8.

53. For the Spirit as down payment or guarantee (Greek, *arrabōn*), see 2 Cor. 1:22; 5:5.

circumstances directly through miraculous signs and wonders (e.g., Rom. 15:19), which, while they often function for Paul as epistemic justification for the content of the preaching that they accompany (e.g., 1 Cor. 2:4–5; Gal. 3:5; 1 Thess. 1:5), are first and foremost expressions of divine grace and aim, as in the ministry of Jesus, to relieve deleterious circumstances.

The proleptic true life is equally marked by transformations of *human relationships*: freedom for the captives (1 Cor. 7:22; Philem. 16), honor extended to the margins (1 Cor. 12:23–24), reconciliation (between people groups and between individuals) and its attendant fruit: unity in the body of Christ. Reconciliation is perhaps the central feature of flourishing circumstances under present conditions (2 Cor. 5:18–20). The hallmark of the peace of proleptic flourishing life should be individuals and people groups truthfully reconciled to one another and living in harmony: worshiping together in the church and seeking the common good in public life.[54]

Transformation of our *relationship with the creation* and the *material goods* God provides through the creation is also a signature of proleptic flourishing. Because "the earth and its fullness are the Lord's" (1 Cor. 10:26), material goods are significant for Paul. And because material provision is a good, Paul is concerned for its equitable distribution.[55] Remembering the poor is the centerpiece of

54. And the opposite is true: the lack of reconciliation is evidence for Paul that the Corinthians are still living "in the flesh"—that is, in the twofold alignment with the unconsummated creation and with sin (1 Cor. 3:3).

55. E.g., 2 Cor. 8:13–15. L. L. Welborn argues persuasively for the centrality of Paul's concern for equity—and its significance for contemporary theological interpretation of Paul—in his review of Bruce Longenecker's *Remember the Poor: Paul, Poverty, and the Greco-Roman Worlds*, in the *Review of Biblical Literature* (2012). This concern for equity is a feature of life in the time between the times. Because sin has made material flourishing a competitive good (in this world—unlike the eschatological vision—some flourish at the expense of others), the pursuit of *peace* in the true life lived under the conditions of the false has to attend specially to issues of inequality. Recognition of the importance of material goods ought to train our eyes to recognize when the "have nots" are humiliated (1 Cor. 11:22) and encourage us to act for the sake of equitable peace, lest we eat and drink judgment on ourselves (11:29).

the decision of the Jerusalem Council as Paul tells it (Gal. 2:10), a key component of Paul's summary of the Jewish law in the love of neighbor, and a cornerstone of his collection for the poor in Jerusalem.[56] That said, we get our relationship to the creation wrong if we begin to think that the flourishing life, even in its circumstantial dimension, is *reducible* to material goods. This is the deeper significance of Paul's insistence that "the kingdom of God is not food and drink" in Romans 14:17. Of course, this assertion is a response to the pressing pastoral question about meat sacrificed to idols. But the statement that the kingdom of God is not food and drink is also a denial of a competing vision of flourishing that would reduce all of life to circumstances alone—and even then, a narrow understanding of only a small subset of circumstances. Paul sees a world full of people living lives oriented around this vision: those whose "god is their belly" (Phil. 3:19), who live merely for the sake of their appetites (Rom. 16:18). This vision is, of course, prevalent in our own day, and the Christian answer is not to *deny* the significance of worldly goods, but rather to understand them within a holistic vision of the world as the good creation of God being renewed as it is drawn to consummation. In this new creation coming to be in our midst, food and drink are not only justly distributed but also revealed as more than just themselves, as God's gifts, as sites of the manifestation of the kingdom. The primary Pauline example is the Eucharist, so long as we are able to discern the true significance of the bread, of the cup, and of the body (of Christ) in our midst.[57]

While the full flourishing peace of the eschaton is a goal toward which we orient our lives, it is also that for the sake of which we

56. While we would be remiss not to acknowledge the role that this collection plays for Paul in the unfolding of the turning of the ages (the wealth of the nations flowing to Zion [Isa. 60:5]; after all, Rom. 15:27 seems to indicate that there is more than mere charitable concern driving the collection), we must also recognize that this verse identifies a significant part of the Jewish law—care for the poor—and places it at the heart of Paul's summary of that law for the gentiles in *love of neighbor*.

57. See 1 Cor. 11:17–34. The concern in 1 Cor. 11 is about how the inequitable distribution of material goods threatens to undermine the unity of the Corinthian church.

often must forgo peace in the here and now. Adherence to the way of love will often bring not the glory that will attend it in the end,[58] but rather opposition that will prevent proleptic life from ever being perfectly at peace. The wisdom of God will appear as foolishness to the world. The power of God will look like weakness. Reconciling peoples will elicit opposition from those who benefit from structures of enmity and division. Pursuing equity of access to material goods will draw the ire of those who profit from existing inequalities. The love of this world is a love that struggles; the circumstances of a life following Jesus will always bear the marks of that struggle. It is the pagan Roman propagandists—not the Christians—whose slogan is "peace and security."[59] Paul's habit is to boast, rather, in the scale and scope of the opposition his ministry has elicited. Outside the context of God's reign fully realized, dire circumstances can offer evidence of flourishing agency (e.g., 2 Cor. 11:23–33). Any hope that we will one day share in the glory of Christ's consummated kingdom comes hand in hand with the expectation that, this side of the God of peace crushing Satan underfoot (Rom. 16:20), we will share in Christ's sufferings (Rom. 8:17; Phil. 3:10–11).

That the proleptic flourishing life is, at many times, manifestly *not* a life of peace demonstrates quite clearly the primacy of love

58. Perhaps no single word is more typical of Paul's descriptions of the age to come than "glory." With this term, Paul emphasizes that, in contrast to the proleptic flourishing life lived under the reign of anti-God powers, the eschatological flourishing life—because it is lived under the rule of God—is one in which the life of love is honored (Rom. 2:10).

59. For a recent summary of the evidence for such a slogan, see Jeffrey A. D. Weima, "'Peace and Security' (1 Thess. 5.3): Prophetic Warning or Political Propaganda?," *New Testament Studies* 58, no. 3 (2012): 331–59. Joel R. White has challenged the consensus view that "*pax et securitas*" amounts to a recognizable imperial slogan as early as the time of Paul. See Joel R. White, "'Peace and Security' (1 Thess. 5.3): Is It Really a Roman Slogan?," *New Testament Studies* 59, no. 3 (2013): 382–95. However, even if one accepts White's correction, he still sees in the phrase the cultural expectations of Roman (*pax*) and Greek (*asphaleia*, security) political thought. See Joel R. White, "'Peace' and 'Security' (1 Thess. 5.3): Roman Ideology and Greek Aspiration," *New Testament Studies* 60, no. 4 (2014): 499–510.

in the Christian life. Peace is not always promised us in the present (Paul has learned to be content in each and every situation), but love is nevertheless commanded: "If it is possible, so far as it depends on you, live peaceably with all" (Rom. 12:18). The true life is not always a life at peace, but is always a life lived for the sake of peace.

Life Feeling as It Should

As, for Paul, agency flourishes in the righteousness of love, and flourishing circumstances are marked by peace, so the distinctive feature of affective flourishing is *joy*. Joy is invoked more frequently in the undisputed Pauline Epistles than in any other body of New Testament literature.[60] Five times in Paul's letters, he commands his hearers to rejoice (2 Cor. 13:11; Phil. 2:18; 3:1; 4:4; 1 Thess. 5:16). Indeed, joy was so central to Paul's ministry that he could use the word to describe that for the sake of which he worked: "We are colaborers of your joy [*synergoi esmen tēs charas hymōn*]" (2 Cor. 1:24).[61] For Paul, joy attends peace and love; it is how love feels when it truly finds itself at peace.

True joy requires an intentional object over which one ought rightly to rejoice,[62] and the superlative "object"—the superlative *cause*—of Christian joy is the presence of God. The paradigmatic command to rejoice is to do so "in the Lord."[63] Even when the prox-

60. Variations of joy (*chara*) and rejoice (*chairō*) occur 46 times in the undisputed Pauline Epistles (Romans, 1–2 Corinthians, Galatians, Philippians, 1 Thessalonians, and Philemon), appearing at a rate of 1.95 times per 1,000 words. The appearance rate for the disputed Pauline Epistles (Ephesians, Colossians, 2 Thessalonians, 1–2 Timothy, Titus) is 0.46; for the Gospels, 0.82; for Acts, 0.60; for the Catholic Epistles (James, 1–2 Peter, 1–3 John, Jude), 1.71; for the Johannine literature (John, 1–3 John), 1.31; for Hebrews, 0.81; and for Revelation, 0.20.

61. Authors' translation.

62. Here we follow Robert Roberts, *Emotions: An Essay in Aid of Moral Psychology* (New York: Cambridge University Press, 2003), 61. To be clear, we do not read Roberts as advocating for a purely "cognitivist" approach to emotions. Affect is an irreducible component of emotion. One cannot be joyful apart from *feeling* joyful, but neither can one rejoice without rejoicing *over* something one has *construed* as being as it ought to be.

63. Phil. 3:1; 4:4; cf. 1 Thess. 3:9. We can expand this set of references by noting that rejoicing "in hope" contains an oblique reference to a divine cause for

imate cause is someone or something else, rejoicing nevertheless happens "in the Lord."[64] The omnipresence of this divine cause for joy makes sense of Paul's command to rejoice always. Unceasing joy is tied to unceasing cultivation of the awareness of—and appropriate response to—the presence of God: continuous prayer and thanksgiving.[65]

As central a cause of joy as God is, most commonly in the Pauline Epistles, the proximate object of joy is other *people*. Again and again, the cause (or, indeed, hoped-for cause) of joy is relational peace between people or their agential flourishing in love.[66] The uniquely Pauline phrase "joy and crown" (Phil. 4:1; 1 Thess. 2:19) captures the intimate connection between joy and human relationship. The members of Paul's churches are *themselves* Paul's joy and his reward. They are so central a cause of joy for Paul that they can be equated with joy itself—even the consummated joy Paul expects as reward for finishing the race he has begun. Because joy is so often tied to relationships, it is to be shared (e.g., Rom. 12:15; 2 Cor. 2:3; Phil. 2:17–18).

At the final consummation, joy characterizes the flourishing of the world that has become the home of God. Because this is the world of perfect love and peace, joy always has objects over which to truthfully rejoice. Furthermore, because it is the world of perfect love, joy always construes the fully consummated world of love and peace rightly *as* true grounds for joy. The world of perfect love and of perfect peace makes possible flourishing life that is always and only a life of joy.

---

joy, particularly in Romans. (On joy in hope: Rom. 12:12; 15:13; on the divine referent of hope: 5:2, 5; 8:20, 24.)

64. E.g., Phil. 4:10: "I rejoice in the Lord greatly that now at last you have revived your concern for me."

65. So 1 Thess. 5:16–18: "Rejoice always, pray without ceasing, give thanks in all circumstances; for this is the will of God in Christ Jesus for you."

66. For relational peace as the grounds for rejoicing, see 2 Cor. 7:4, 7; Phil. 2:2; 4:1; 1 Thess. 2:19–20; 3:9. For agential flourishing as the grounds for joy, see Rom. 16:19 (where Paul rejoices over the recipients' obedience); 2 Cor. 7:9 (where Paul rejoices in response to the Corinthians' repentance); and Philem. 7 (where Paul says he has much joy and encouragement on account of Philemon's love).

As in the case of peace, the proleptic flourishing life is not always and *only* a life of joy. And, again in parallel to the case of peace, part of what prevents it from being so is the primacy of love. Because love is anchored in the truth,[67] living *into* fully consummated joy, while grounded in love, we have emotional lives that are normed by truthful construal of the world around us. The proleptic flourishing life sees rightly and is emotionally present to the world as it actually is. For this reason, this life is marked not just by joy but also by sorrow (and by anger). *Lament* is a crucial truthful practice of the kingdom under present conditions—especially within the body of Christ. Because affect is, for Paul, *bodily* (as it is anew for modern psychology!), life in the body of Christ involves sharing the affective life of the members of the body. While, with an eye toward the nearness of God, the rule is to "rejoice always," with regard to ecclesial relations, the rule is instead to "rejoice with those who rejoice; mourn with those who mourn" (Rom. 12:15 NIV).[68] The proleptic life is lived between these two commands: the command to rejoice always in light of God's nearness and the command to *feel* life honestly and in unity with those to whom one has been called to live in peace. When Paul's gaze turns to the world in its form that is passing away, the picture becomes even more complex, and he finds himself having to speak in paradoxical terms: "[Let] those who mourn [be] as though they were not mourning, and those who rejoice as though they were not rejoicing" (1 Cor. 7:30).[69] Because the world

67. 1 Cor. 13:6: "[Love] does not rejoice in wrongdoing, but rejoices in the truth."

68. We use the NIV here in order to highlight the verbal resonance with 1 Cor. 7:30 below, where the verb is again *klaiō* and the NRSV and NIV both translate this as "mourn." The somatic logic is plain in 1 Cor. 12:26: "If one member suffers, all suffer together with it; if one member is honored, all rejoice together with it."

69. One could read Paul's hesitancy in 1 Cor. 7:30 as having to do with the same somatic logic that structures Rom. 12:15. In both cases, the foundational principle is that somatic unity and affective participation go hand in hand. In 1 Cor. 7:30, however, the threat is that intimate affective alignment with the world in its present form would lead to somatic unity with this *other body* that is now coming to nothing (Rom. 6:6).

is subject to corruption and under the dominion of Sin, affective alignment with it is a dangerous business.

Under the conditions of sin, much of what passes for "joy" is false or corrupt. Witness, for example, our lives on social media, where we regularly rejoice over those who mourn (Twitter's schadenfreude) and mourn over those who rejoice (Facebook's envy and "fear of missing out," or FOMO). For biblical examples, we might consider the joy of the chief priests and temple guard as they greet Judas's betrayal (Luke 22:5) and Herod's joy as he greets the Christ in chains (23:8). All three aspects of Paul's definition of the kingdom—righteousness, peace, and joy—are parodied by the enemies of the gospel. The Pharisees champion (self-) righteousness. The Romans trumpet "peace and security." The ruling Judean elites revel in counterfeit joy as Jesus is betrayed, tried, and executed. Paul recognizes the possibility of perverse joys and the role that love plays in keeping joy situated on a firm foundation of truth when he insists that love "does not rejoice in wrongdoing, but rejoices in the truth" (1 Cor. 13:6).

Its perils notwithstanding, affect can itself be a locus of the kingdom's irruption in the midst of the false life of the present world. In fixing the community's gaze on God, joy can become a collective practice of *resistance*. Precisely as joy *contra mundi*, joy can function not as a naïve but rather as a purposeful rejection of the sinful conditions of the false life. Joy can be a communal statement that true life is guaranteed eschatologically, and, in this life, true life is both possible and, in ways enduring but impure, coming to be in the midst of the false.[70] Because of this tension, on this side of the eschaton, joy and sorrow intermix. Proleptic joy must always leave room for sorrow, even as, in sorrow, we leave room for joy. We need to be able to rejoice over proleptic manifestations of the kingdom and the eschatological banquet of which they offer a foretaste. But, given the holism of the Christian vision

---

70. Willie James Jennings outlined the significance of joy *contra mundi* in "Joy That Gathers," a paper presented at a consultation at the Yale Center for Faith and Culture, New Haven, CT, August 21–22, 2014.

of flourishing life, our joy over a small part of the world at peace will always contain within it a mourning over the fact that this island of peace is not yet integrated into a whole world at peace. Finally, in this life, Paul is clear that we rejoice not only in spite of suffering but also, in certain cases, because of it (Rom. 5:3–5). When suffering is a result—and therefore a sign—of our love having elicited the inevitable opposition that genuine love under present conditions generates, then our suffering, as evidence of love oriented toward peace, is precisely a ground for joy. The joy that comes from sharing in Christ's suffering is not a masochistic delight in suffering itself, but rather an encouragement taken from recognizing Christ's love being lived through us and yielding its characteristic, but nevertheless ironic, fruit. This joy in suffering points to a yet greater joy in a world in which the love that now suffers finds its fitting home and reveals itself as a love that reigns together.

Flourishing Life as Gift

Let us not miss the crucial phrase "in the Holy Spirit." This phrase extends to all three aspects of Paul's definition, not just to joy.[71] And it is not just here in Romans that Paul points to the importance of the Spirit for all three aspects of the good life. First and foremost, the Spirit is the source of the love of God that is the root of all flourishing life. "Our hope of sharing the glory of God" is on account of "God's love [having] been poured into our hearts through the Holy Spirit" (Rom. 5:2, 5). The Spirit's presence and

71. Here we follow Käsemann, *Commentary on Romans*, 377; Ulrich Wilckens, *Der Brief an die Römer*, vol. 3, Evangelische-katholischer Kommentar zum Neuen Testamentum 6 (Zurich: Benziger, 1978–82), 92; Joseph A. Fitzmyer, *Romans: A New Translation with Introduction and Commentary*, Anchor Bible 33 (New York: Doubleday, 1993), 697; Douglas J. Moo, *The Epistle to the Romans*, New International Commentary on the New Testament (Grand Rapids: Eerdmans, 1996), 857; against Robert Jewett, *Romans: A Commentary*, Hermeneia (Minneapolis: Fortress Press, 2007), 863; Theodor Zahn, *Der Brief des Paulus an die Römer*, Kommentar zum Neuen Testament 6 (Leipzig: Deichert, 1910), 581; Otto Michel, *Der Brief an die Römer*, 14th ed., Kritische-exegetischer Kommentar über das Neues Testament 4 (Göttingen: Vandenhoeck & Ruprecht, 1978), 435.

agency are also key to the proleptic realization of the eschatological kingdom. Communicating the love of God, the Spirit bears fruit of "love, joy, [and] peace" in our lives (Gal. 5:22).[72] The Spirit is a down payment, generator of the firstfruits and a guarantee of God's promised harvest, a bearer of the presence of the future.

The flourishing life, on the Christian account, is a life lived through the agency of God and in the presence of God. It is in this sense that we insist that the "kingdom of God" and the "home of God" are metaphors for two sides of the same reality. The kingdom is where and when God rules in such a way as to make the world fit in its entirety to be God's home and therefore humanity's true home as well. Each of the three aspects of the good life points at this "intimacy" of God and the world. Righteousness is possible only because through the Spirit, divine love has poured into our hearts (Rom. 5:5) or because Christ lives in us, and through his indwelling we, in turn, live "in" Christ and participate in *his* life. Even as we insist that righteousness is not a mere legal fiction but rather the shape of a life normed by the law of love, we must equally insist that it is not the accomplishment of the diligent believer, but rather a free *gift* of grace.[73] Peace in human affairs and of the creation as a whole is born of the reality of God's liberative action and presence. Joy is, first and foremost, a fruit

72. We might also note that these same three are promised by Jesus in John's farewell discourse—peace in 14:27, love in 15:9–10, and joy in 15:11—sandwiched between promises of the sending of the Spirit of truth (14:17, 26; 15:26; 16:13).

73. Romans 5:17 asserts quite plainly that righteousness is a gift: "If, because of the one man's trespass, death exercised dominion through that one, much more surely will those who receive the abundance of grace and the free gift of righteousness exercise dominion in life through the one man, Jesus Christ." 1 Corinthians 6:11 interweaves the agency of Christ and that of the Spirit in typically Pauline fashion, describing the Corinthians as having been "justified in the name of the Lord Jesus Christ and in the Spirit of our God." The contrast between possible sources of righteousness is one of the main themes of Galatians but is stated perhaps most straightforwardly in Phil. 3:9, where Paul describes himself as "not having a righteousness of [his] own that comes from the law, but one that comes through faith in Christ [*dia pisteōs Christou*], the righteousness from God based on faith." Whether we translate *pistis Christou* as "faith in Christ," as does the NRSV, or as "faithfulness of Christ" makes no difference on this point. In either case, righteousness comes otherwise than by our own moral exertion.

of the Spirit, whether we are rejoicing in the goods of this world or in God. Each aspect of the flourishing life—each dimension of the kingdom—is a gift from God—and a gift that does not come by some heavenly post from a distance, but one that is tied to the agency and very presence of God.

The Interdependence of Righteousness, Peace, and Joy

While Paul lists righteousness, peace, and joy in sequence—and we have taken them up in a similar way—they are not independent. Rather, as we have already begun to see, they are perichoretic, interpenetrating in at least two senses.

First, you can't have any one of the three in its fullness without the other two. It is impossible to enact an entirely flourishing human agency—to act rightly—in corrupt circumstances.[74] Even were *sin* (*per impossibile!*) avoided, apart from flourishing circumstances, righteousness would lie unfulfilled, for fully flourishing human agency involves *cooperation* with a world of flourishing agents—right relationship with genuinely righteous people.[75] It is equally impossible to enact an entirely flourishing human agency apart from the joy that makes one love the law of love.[76] Abundant joy overflows in acts of love that bring about peace.[77] Likewise, it is impossible to have a world truly at peace apart from flour-

74. Consider the example of the way that Sin corrupts the law and uses it to bring about death (Rom. 7:11) in the case of racial bias, police violence, and the just law of self-defense. See Croasmun, *Emergence of Sin*, 127–28.

75. Paul makes this point in the reverse when he warns that "bad company ruins good morals" (1 Cor. 15:33).

76. So Aquinas, *In ad Rom.* C.14 L.2, 1128: "Joy must be referred to the manner in which the works of justice are to be accomplished; for as the Philosopher says in book one of the Ethics, a man is not just who does not take joy in acts of justice. Hence a psalm says: serve the Lord with gladness (Ps. 100:2)."

In the Pauline Epistles themselves, one might point to Phil. 3:1, in which the command to "rejoice in the Lord" functions as a thesis statement for the ensuing section of the letter, which offers ethical instructions. The key to living rightly is to rejoice in the Lord, rather than in "the flesh."

77. For example, regarding the churches of Macedonia: "During a severe ordeal of affliction, their abundant joy and their extreme poverty have overflowed in a wealth of generosity on their part" (2 Cor. 8:2).

ishing agency[78] and without recognition of the world as what it is—namely, a gift from God. That act of recognition is a vital component of flourishing agency, and the sense of gratitude that accompanies it is no less vital a component of flourishing affect. Furthermore, among the circumstances we most desire is an environment, a community, a world that is in some sense in a state of joy. A world stocked with every good *thing* but bereft of joy is a world not yet fully at peace. And, finally, it is impossible to have true joy apart from justice and peace. It is possible, as we have noted, to rejoice over injustice—whether perpetrated by us or by another—but this is a corrupt joy. It is similarly possible to rejoice in willful ignorance of the dire circumstances of one's neighbor, but this is a selfish and indifferent joy. On the other hand, it is possible to cultivate genuine joy in the face of lamentable circumstances and to rejoice *contra mundi* precisely as a mode of resistance to injustice, but these joys always have some character of a "bright sorrow"[79] and point beyond themselves in hope of the joy of the consummated kingdom. Fully realized, joy is the affective fruit of true peace born of love.

Second, the three terms themselves—love, peace, and joy (here, we perform the substitution Paul is happy to make in Galatians)—exhibit a perichoretic relationship, having secondary and tertiary senses that overlap with the domains of the other two. So, while love has to do with flourishing agency, Paul can lean on the word as the foundation on which an entire new world is founded.[80] Yet more rarely, the concept can denote an affective state, the sort of love that Paul places in apposition to "longing" in Philippians 4:1.[81] Similarly, while peace primarily denotes a state of affairs, it

78. So Aquinas, *In ad Rom.* C.14 L.2, 1128: "Peace refers to the effect of justice."

79. Alexander Schmemann, *The Journals of Father Alexander Schmemann, 1973–1983*, trans. Julianna Schmemann (Crestwood, NY: St. Vladimir's Seminary Press, 2000), 137.

80. See, e.g., Rom. 8:35, 39; 1 Cor. 13.

81. We might also think of Aquinas's point about the way that certain affective postures motivate right action. Indeed, if we take *love* to define the content of the agential aspect of the flourishing life, at least in contemporary English, this tertiary affective sense would be quite prominent; it is hard to imagine fully

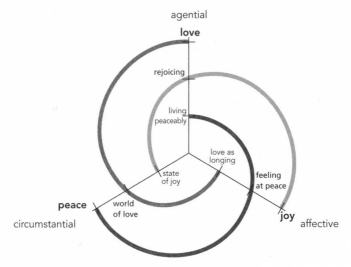

Figure 6.1 The perichoresis of love, peace, and joy.

can often also describe an internal state—a feeling—that has to do primarily with the heart and mind.[82] Yet more rarely, it is possible for Paul to speak of "living peaceably [*eirēneuontes*]" (Rom. 12:18), reminding us that peace also includes a latent *agential* aspect. Finally, the joy we *feel* can become an act we choose, as in the many places we are commanded to rejoice, and can thereby become a continual state "in the Lord," to which the believer can always return (e.g., Phil. 4:4; 1 Thess. 5:16).

—— Articulate, Discern, and Commend the Vision ——

In this concluding chapter we have sketched a vision of the flourishing life by thinking theologically with the apostle Paul. With a

loving someone—even in the active sense that *agapē* always retains—without being moved affectively in some way.

82. E.g., Phil. 4:7: "And the peace of God, which surpasses all understanding, will guard your hearts and your minds in Christ Jesus."

slightly different result, we could have done the same by engaging one of the Synoptic Gospels or the Johannine corpus. Such a vision of flourishing, whether based on the writings of a single biblical author or on all of them together, is not yet a full-fledged theology of flourishing life, though it is a step toward it. A theology of flourishing life would require much more comprehensive engagement with the whole range of Christian convictions, from the nature of God to the character of the world to come, equivalent in scope to the work of the great theologians of the church from the past. We hope that our theologizing about flourishing life with Paul will spur others—from biblical scholars and historians of religion to constructive and practical theologians and everyone in between—to make articulating, discerning, and commending a vision of flourishing life the main purpose of their work, and to do so even when such a vision is not their main focus.

In a keynote address to the American Academy of Religion about the nature of theology (1994), Jürgen Moltmann said, "It is simple, but true, to say that theology has only one single problem: God. We are theologians for the sake of God. God is our dignity. God is our agony. God is our hope."[83] But though we are theologians for God's sake, we are not theologians for God's benefit. God doesn't need theology. If anyone needs it, human beings do. Let us be theologians for the sake of the life, the *true* life, of the world.

---

83. Jürgen Moltmann, *Theology and the Future of the Modern World* (Pittsburgh: ATS, 1995), 1.

Acknowledgments

The central idea of this book came into focus when, after reading Anthony Kronman's book *Education's End* (2008),[1] Miroslav realized that a key source of the current crisis in theology is the malady afflicting higher education more broadly: a systematic marginalization of the question of the true and truly flourishing life. He articulated the idea first in a lecture titled "Life Worth Living: The Christian Faith and the Crisis of the Humanities," which he gave at Oxford University during a conference on Christianity and the Flourishing of Universities (May 2012, organized with the support of the McDonald Agape Foundation).[2] The book itself began as a manifesto in outline form that Miroslav first prepared for a lecture at the Louisville Institute's Vocation of the Theological Educator program at their winter seminar for doctoral and postdoctoral fellows in February 2015. A month later, in March 2015, he discussed the lecture with a small gathering of researchers at the Yale Center for Faith and Culture: Ryan Darr,

1. Anthony Kronman, *Education's End: Why Our Colleges and Universities Have Given Up on the Meaning of Life* (New Haven: Yale University Press, 2007).
2. Miroslav Volf, "Life Worth Living: The Christian Faith and the Crisis of the Humanities," presented at the McDonald Centre conference on Christianity and the Flourishing of Universities, Oxford, UK, May 24–25, 2012, https://faith.yale.edu/sites/default/files/life_worth_living-volf.pdf.

Janna Gonwa, and Ryan McAnnally-Linz, all doctoral students at the time. These two groups of young theologians offered the very first responses to the proposal, both critical and affirmative—and provided the impetus for filling out the original rough sketch of the renewal of theology.

The generous support of the John Templeton Foundation for the Center's three-year project on Theology of Joy and the Good Life allowed us to gather a number of theologians (and nontheologians!) to offer critical feedback along the way. In October 2015, Barbara Hallensleben, Willie James Jennings, George Marsden, Tyler Roberts, Casey Strine, and Guido Vergauwen, each coming from their own subfields within theology and religious studies, provided a crucial first round of feedback on the broad arc of our proposal. In February 2016, Michal Beth Dinkler, Amy Hughes, Stephen Moore, Fernando Segovia, and Francis Watson sharpened our thinking about our proposal as it relates to biblical studies and the study of ancient Christianity.

In April 2016, Justin Crisp, Keri Day, Adam Eitel, Eric Gregory, and Bethany Joy Kim helped us think about the question of alignment of the theologian's work with her life. Justin, a doctoral student at Yale and a researcher at the Center for more than five years, prepared a text on the relation between spirituality and theology in contemporary theology. His position resonated so much with our own that he, an extraordinary thinker and also a priest, became a coauthor of the chapter on the relation between theologians' lives and theological work. In addition to coauthoring that chapter, he served diligently as a researcher, providing briefs on far-ranging topics—including one that ultimately produced the note on the theological importance of the question of angels dancing on the head of a pin, a favorite of many readers of early drafts. In June 2016, Peter Bouteneff, Luke Bretherton, Katie Grimes, Alan Mittleman, Katherine Sonderegger, and Graham Tomlin helped us tackle the challenge of doing this sort of Christian theology in pluralistic contexts.

In between gatherings with these exceptional scholars from beyond our institution, we were also fortunate to get invaluable feedback on early drafts from Yale faculty and doctoral students in theology, philosophy of religion, ethics, biblical studies, and ancient Christianity who participated in colloquia focused on our developing text. Adam Eitel in particular has been an important dialogue partner; the conversation with Thomas Aquinas that runs through much of this book is due in large part to Adam's erudition and passion for this book's ideas.

We should also thank our friends and colleagues at the University of Fribourg, where Miroslav presented and discussed the outline of the manifesto in June 2015 and where Matt gave a series of lectures on the project in October 2016 to their ecumenical student body, Catholic, Protestant, Orthodox, and Evangelical. Barbara Hallensleben and Guido Vergauwen, as we mentioned, were partners from the start. Walter Dürr has worked tirelessly to build the collaboration. We are grateful for their partnership.

In the summer of 2017, Matt and Miroslav each presented drafts of what became chapters of this book at the annual conference of the Society of Vineyard Scholars and received valuable input from the scholars in that community. Later that same summer, Daniel Aleshire, former president of the Association of Theological Schools, generously provided constructive comments on our account of the "external crisis" facing theology, helping us grasp more fully and precisely the state of theological education in the United States and Canada—including highlighting a number of encouraging signs that have tempered our somewhat grim account.

In February 2018 we had a chance to present a draft of chapter 6 to a group of scholars of non-Christian religious and philosophical traditions. We are so grateful to Ismail Fajrie Alatas, Yonatan Brafman, Robert Emmons, Philip J. Ivanhoe, Jeffrey Hopkins, Richard Tail Kim, Katarzyna de Lazari, Alan Mittleman, Anthony Pinn, Anantanand Rambachan, Roxanne Rashedi, and Jongbok Yi for their wisdom and insight as we envision the good life Christianly in our pluralistic world.

We are immensely grateful to all these many scholars from diverse contexts for investing their time and their considerable intellect in engaging with the ideas in this book and especially for the pushback against its ideas. The final product is far the better for their protests and resistance, even when at times we chose not to move the text in the direction they urged. We are grateful for their insights, but we should also be clear: these fine folks should in no sense be held responsible for what we have to say here.

Throughout the project, the entire team at the Yale Center for Faith and Culture has wrestled with and worked within the framework we lay out here. It has been a joy to write this book *about* doing theology centered on the question of the good life while at the same time *doing* theology just this way alongside brilliant and faithful colleagues. Theology of this sort is best as a team enterprise, and we are especially grateful to Drew Collins, Sarah Farmer, Angela Gorrell, and Ryan McAnnally-Linz, who have been our daily collaborators over these three years. Ryan is something of a silent coauthor of this book, as he is for just about anything either of us writes these days.

We also benefited tremendously from the labor of a number of student researchers. Janna Gonwa provided copious research for many of the sprawling areas of inquiry into which this project spills, including helping thoughtfully frame the relationship between theology and religious studies, assertion and violence, and other topics. Nathan Jowers ably assisted Matt with exegetical research for chapter 6, demonstrating theological insight and exegetical skill beyond his years. Ryan Ramsey helped get this manuscript "across the finish line," working tirelessly under tight deadlines to clean up references and find answers to far-ranging research questions.

The title of our book is itself something for which we owe someone thanks and acknowledgement. *For the Life of the World* is a small but extraordinary book that Alexander Schmemann published over half a century ago (1963). We borrowed the title because, in our own way, we share both Schmemann's sacramental vision of the world as the site of communion with God and his opposition to either seeking refuge from the world in God alone or to employing God as tool to improve the world according to our own preset plan.

From Miroslav: In addition to those we already mentioned, I owe a debt of gratitude to two sets of people for their contribution to this book, those from far away and those at home. I have presented ideas contained in this book to many audiences, most recently in Sydney (Center for Public Christianity, 2015); Atlanta (American Academy of Religion, 2015, and Emory University, 2016); Moscow (Postgraduate School of Russian Orthodox Church, 2015); Copenhagen (University of Copenhagen, 2016); Minneapolis (University of Minnesota, 2017); Boston (Boston College, 2017); Lakeland (Florida Southern College, 2017); San Diego (University of San Diego, 2018); Conway, Arkansas (Hendrix College, 2018); and Seoul, South Korea (Underwood Lectures, as well as lectures at Yonsei University and Presbyterian College and Theological Seminary, 2018). I am grateful for the engagement of these diverse publics with the vision of theology I presented and for their contribution to my thinking about it. At home, my wife, Jessica, whose rigorous and beautiful mind is a daily source of delight, has been unfailingly supportive of my work on this book, catching many balls that I dropped when I was either away at speaking engagements or at home but in "the book world" mentally. I dedicate this book—my contribution to it—to Mira Frances, our daughter, who was born four months before the draft of the book was completed. To my surprise, she energized the final months of writing by nothing more than the reality of her delightful and distracting presence. As a newborn, she became for me a symbol of what this book is largely about: life that comes to be and flourishes in the environment of God's life-giving presence, and life that is as such a source of joy.

From Matt: My theological home for going on twelve years has been the Elm City Vineyard Church; that community has meant so much to me as we have struggled together to do theology and live our lives for the sake of the life of our city. The best practices of that community are always smarter than the best of my ideas. The Vineyard community in Germany, Austria, and Switzerland has also contributed importantly to this project, inviting me to speak about the theology of the good life in Berlin in January 2018 and offering a glimpse of the possible fruit of this sort of theology if embraced in the church. I cannot fully express my profound gratitude to my parents, who instilled a love of theology, imparted a vision of flourishing that is more than bread alone, and, day in and day out, make possible the simultaneous flourishing of my work *and* my family. My wife, Hannah, has been a theological colaborer ever since we met in a study of the Gospel of Mark our first year in college. This book, like everything else I do, would not exist without her love and support. Junia Ruth, to whom my contribution to this book is dedicated, continues to be Hannah's and my joy, our own precious site of hope for flourishing life in and for the world.

This publication was made possible through support from the John Templeton and McDonald Agape foundations. The opinions expressed in this publication are those of the authors and do not necessarily reflect the views of the two foundations.

Index